You Are
God
Enough

You Are GOD Enough

Conversations with
the Holy Spirit on
Manifesting
Your Purpose

Stevie Ray McHugh

You Are God Enough:
Conversations with the Holy Spirit
on Manifesting Your Purpose

Copyright © 2016 Steven Raymond McHugh

For information contact :
http://www.StevieRayMcHugh.com

Editing & interior design by:
www.WordNinjaServices.com
Cover design by: www.KenBernstein.com
Photos of Stevie Ray by Kate Zari Roberts.
ISBN: 978-1537284033

First Edition: October 2016

For my mother

We are never apart.

Acknowledgments

First and foremost, I would like to acknowledge the being I have come to call Aion. Your powerful appearance in my life and ongoing transmissions have uplifted and transformed me in ways I could never have imagined. I am forever grateful for your guidance, wisdom, and support.

Thank you to my first spiritual teacher, Prem Rawat, whom I knew as Guru Maharaj Ji, for putting me on the spiritual path so many years ago. Meeting you saved my life.

Heartfelt gratitude to Michelle Williams of *WordNinjaServices.com* for your amazing love, support, and talents as a writer, editor, and book consultant. Your persistence and patience with my resistance, your humor, deep wisdom, and brilliant insights have continued to inspire me. I never would have finished this book without you.

Special thanks to Michael Powell, Mitchell Ditkoff, and Ria Moran. Your friendship and feedback on this project kept me going when my own doubts would have stopped me. I am forever grateful.

To Jeff Salzman, Ross Hostetter, Keith Martin-Smith, and Katy Koontz, you have been a top-notch coaching squad that made all the difference in my game. Deep gratitude to Mary, whose radiant heart light and inspired instruction opened me to receiving guidance. And a heartfelt thank you to Doreen Virtue. Without your inspired book, *Divine Guidance*, mine would never have happened.

Last but certainly not least, thank you to the loving crew of folks such as Olivia Parr-Rudd, Adelyn Jones, Tom Hansen, Henri Koshen Czechorowski, Helen Knight, Joni Goering, and Chris Menné for your enthusiastic participation in the Unified Field Work with Aion. Your willingness to allow this work to touch you has forever touched me.

CONTENTS

Introduction

I never intended to write a book. As early as high school, I found writing a frustrating chore. I had far too many ideas and saw too many links between them to even know where to begin. After starting, my mind spidered out in a hundred directions at once, making the task of organizing my thoughts on paper an exercise in futility. To complicate matters, I am dyslexic, a condition that used to make spelling and typing an excruciating ordeal. The day I gave away my Smith-Corona and left college truly was a happy one.

So what changed? During the first transmission of this book, messages came through me in the mildly disassociated state I describe a few pages from now. The words were not mine in the least. After this first encounter, the process shifted. The transmissions were like being thrown into the middle of an action adventure movie. In the thick of the experience, I could easily describe it as a narrator, giving a blow-by-blow account of unfolding events. But through it all, I have never needed to write, at least not in the traditional sense. A stream of language has carried me forward, words flowing out of me with no effort on my part.

Through this process, the energies coming through me also taught me to type. Believe me, I know that sounds a bit far-fetched. But the first time I received these energy messages, I was watching my fingers type perfectly, despite the fact that I had literally never learned this skill. That alone was a miracle, no matter what the words coming through me had to say. Soon, receiving a transmission was less like being taken over and more like serving as a translator. But somehow my fingers remembered how to move over the keys. It was the fastest business class I ever took.

The truth is, I am not a writer, but a messenger. From the beginning, I received very clear guidance to turn the messages I was receiving into a book. Like a good soldier, I labored over the material. I gathered, organized, arranged. I thought and rethought word choices and placement, crafting and honing the content into what seemed to me like a polished gem. I was committed to presenting these messages with clarity and care.

Then I showed my work to others—writers, editors, published authors. All responded positively. Many even loved it, pointing out pithy quotes that had stayed with them or confessing they had cried while reading it. But almost everyone expressed, in one way or another, something was missing.

"Where are you in this book, Stevie?" they would ask. "What was happening in your life when these messages came through?" They wanted context. They wanted my stories.

Stories about me? About my life? Ugh. The downloads had started at the collapse of my business. My marriage would turn south not long after. It had been one of the hardest periods of my life, and I thought the manuscript already exposed too much of the pain and struggle I had experienced. The thought of putting the details of my saga on paper for the world to see made me wince.

My other concern about adding my life's stories to this book was that they might somehow detract from the message I had to share. After all, this book is not an autobiography. It is meant to feature the teaching I received, not my personality, my life stories, or the raw edges of my own process.

In the end, however, the advice of others won me over. The Holy Spirit, referred to as "Aion" through most of this book, sent me a writer and editor who insisted on throwing out all my hard work. I took a deep breath, let go of years of labor and dove in headfirst with her. She went back to the original material and helped me to add my stories. Through interviews, she pulled out of me the personal narrative surrounding my interchanges with the Holy Spirit like unraveling a tangled ball of thread. Together we wove that thread through these pages.

The result is a book much closer to the bone—my bone, anyway. It is the uncensored version of the first six months of my lucid, life-changing conversations with a being I knew first as Aion, along with

Aion's colleagues in Spirit, the Beings of Light and the Soul Guardians. Through these pages, you will journey with me to my sudden, surprising understanding that Aion is actually the Holy Spirit. All the stories from my life in the book are true, and the conversations with the Holy Spirit are very close to the way they first happened for me. I can take no credit for the grace and beauty of the language you will read. The unique perspective it offers has always been both unexpected and spot on for me, clearly beyond the limits of my own small viewpoint.

As you read, you may notice a fair amount of repetition. Clearly I'm a slow learner. I have always been amazed by the degree of patience and willingness I felt from the Holy Spirit through this process. The messages have balanced challenge with patience, drawing me back to a teaching point again and again until I finally reached the aha! Yet not a single word of judgment of me has ever come through in these transmissions. Perhaps this is my biggest clue that these insights are not a product of my own personality.

Hopefully the pun-laced humor in these conversations, which has come through with a flavor and flair aimed originally at my own funny bone, will provide some comic relief for all. But I simply cannot convey in words the loving, soul-attuned energy infusing the transmissions as I experienced them. I must rely on the Holy Spirit to transmit this experience to you.

In this process, I think of myself as the forward scout in an expedition party. I have gone ahead to help others find their way through this territory. This book has the most vulnerable parts of me in it—my heartbreak, my doubt, all my resistance—as well as language that may seem to some a little rough around the edges. I offer this perfectly imperfect version of my story with the intention that you will be able to see your own struggles reflected in mine.

My great ambition for this book? That it will inspire you to open to your own guidance. That you will know beyond a shadow of a doubt that you are never alone. Support surrounds you constantly, just as it has me, guiding the direction your life will take and the progress you make in your journey back to Source. Trust me. If this can happen to me, it can happen to you. You only need ask and practice receiving to find the answers you seek.

A Word on Words

I'm the kind of guy who gets a little antsy about words like God. At some point along the way, I considered leaving that word out of the book altogether, along with a handful of others.

In the end, I kept "God" in the title of the book, knowing that it might bother some readers like me who grew up with the word hanging over them like an ominous thundercloud. I chose to use the word in this way because it comes from Aion in a different spirit than the one I grew up with as a Catholic. In this case, I think Aion's usage turns the old meaning of the word on its head.

When it appears within the book, the word "God" points to the all-powerful force—nameless, faceless, formless—that also, paradoxically, takes form in each of us. It is what some esoteric traditions call the great I Am, the part of a human being that cannot be changed or destroyed.

In the same vein, I have chosen the word Source to refer to this energy in the book, mostly when speaking of it as something that seems outside of us. I say "seems" because Aion and many others have made it clear: God, Source is what we are made from and is never apart from us. We are that divinity.

Another thing I've struggled with is what to call the process I experience of receiving messages from the Holy Spirit. The experience is very different from and so much more vivid than what I have known as prayer. In the end, I believe that understanding my process of receiving this wisdom is far more important than any label I may give it.

The messages come through me as words, feelings, and pictures, along with a stream of uplifting energy sometimes so powerful that I can barely contain it. I receive a flow of intelligence that moves both through and beyond me, something akin to the way the North Sea flows through the English Channel to join the Atlantic Ocean. In the experience, I become both a messenger, translating my experience into words, and an actual energy circuit through which healing energy connects from Spirit to Earth. These waves of healing energy are a phenomenon that I simply cannot put into words.

For me, this is the most important aspect of being a messenger, the element of being a conduit. The exercise is mostly one of getting out of the way so this energy can move, unhindered. Even though I type words, I am not actually writing them, at least not inventing them myself. In fact, I often don't remember what Spirit says through me and have to read the material again later to grasp its full meaning. Opening to this flow has been life-changing. As you might expect, the information coming through has grown my awareness by leaps and bounds; but also, the energy itself, beyond any words, has been a balm to my soul. Basking in that energy, the sheer delight of it, has transformed my entire life.

The truth is, everyone is a messenger of some kind. Of course, it takes different forms for different people. An artist expressing genius nearly always speaks about the process in otherworldly terms—a visitation from the muse, perhaps, or a sense of the art happening *through* instead of *from* the artist. Psychology focused on peak performance states echoes this theme, pointing to heightened awareness as a key feature of high functioning. No matter how we choose to approach it, this work I refer to, the work of bridging Heaven and Earth, is, in a sense, a calling we all share.

My hope, then, is that this material will support others not just to see and understand the Holy Spirit with new eyes, but also to access the flow of higher guidance available at any time to anyone. Serving as a messenger in the way I experience it is a skill that anyone can develop. It starts with the simple practice of quieting the mind and tuning in to the present.

How to Use This Book

One approach is to read this book in the traditional way, from front cover to back. But keep in mind that this is not just my story. If you choose, it can serve as a gateway, a living field of energy to catapult you into your own growth process. Because of this, you can ask for guidance, then open the pages at random and read what jumps out at you. You might even consider working with the book in a group to share and integrate the insights you all receive. If you're like me, you're bound to notice different parts of the material coming forward at different times, based on your needs in the moment.

However you enter the book, the most important thing is to practice the work it presents. The book contains my own experiences, which can serve as a template for you to follow. But there is no substitute for a direct encounter with Aion and the Beings of Light. Whether you rely on these practices or create your own, aim for making contact, both with the Holy Spirit and your Higher Self.

If this notion seems abstract or you find it difficult to believe you can experience it yourself, simply ask Aion and his Gang for help. You will be surprised at the creative and interesting methods this intelligence will use to reach through your limits to bring you forward on your journey. As the Holy Spirit has reminded me again and again, an earnest desire for transformation gets the immediate attention of those beyond the veil.

Along these lines, the promise in this book is that anyone who practices its meditations will have a direct experience of Source. In the main text, the practices I received appear in a loose, conversational format as I first experienced them. The website offers some of them in a more structured form for you to use on a regular basis. These practices help you move into an active, creative relationship with your own Higher Self, the ultimate aim of Soul Integration Work. I can promise that the fruit of your practice will prove well worth the time and energy you invest in it.

This material is alive, backed by the energy and intelligence of Source. I offer it as an aid and guide for you; take what resonates and leave the rest. But the Holy Spirit and the Beings of Light have made it clear: Ask for Spirit's presence and support, and you will receive it. May the wisdom here lead you to follow the path that sparkles.

You Are
God
Enough

I

Making Contact

"The time is now for spreading the word of an ever-increasing vibration of love throughout the world. This is a magical time when all beings can achieve progress on their path to Source."

~The Beings of Light

Lightning. That's the best word I have for the bolt of electricity that shot from my feet, through my legs, up my spine, to the top of my head. Current arced through me as if I had stuck my finger in a wall socket, all my hairs standing on end. I lifted out of my skin, until I was hovering behind myself and up a few feet, looking down at my body. My arms appeared very long, my computer, faraway. And my hands were doing something I had never learned: Typing. Instead of my usual dyslexic hunt-and-peck, my fingers moved deftly across the keys, filling the screen with the smooth motion of words not my own.

What was happening to me? It had started innocently enough, with me sitting down with my laptop and a question. But now, language appeared on the screen without me, the words distant, yet in sharp focus. Energy surged through my body so strongly that I wondered, even as I marveled at it, if I would survive.

It all happened in an instant, one raw moment lifted out of space and time. But in the months and years ahead, I would come to realize it had taken a lifetime to get here, to this one moment that would change me forever.

Risk had become the name of the game for me. Money to the tune of six figures, along with five years of my spare time, had gone into a business metrics software start-up, a venture I created to carry my wife and me into retirement. I had battled my way through my business partner's lack of management experience and my own lack of knowledge in the arena of software development. We poured endless time and energy into the project. But despite all our efforts, we somehow just couldn't finish the last 15 percent of the product.

During this time, I slipped on an old doormat on my back porch, breaking my ankle, toes, and leg. The spiral fracture in my leg went overlooked by doctors and bled into my system, creating blood clots in my lungs. For more than five months, I could not work at all, and focusing on the software company was next to impossible. I was adrift.

But in January 2009, I finally saw dry land. I found a small company with a team of software developers who could finish our product and wanted to buy our business. For me, it was nothing short of a miracle. The sale would mean money in my pocket and a big, full-time job with the purchasing company. I could pay off the mounting debt and put an end to the odyssey I'd been living.

My wife was even more relieved than I was. When we married, I had promised to take care of her financially and later even encouraged her to quit her job to start a seminar company around her own work. But now, after dealing with my injury, I was finding it tough to make ends meet. We truly needed my company to sell. And with this deal, everything was in place. I already had my own clients using the software as it was, and now, I had a buyer.

When the buyer's daughter, just a teenager, died suddenly in a freak accident, we all found ourselves shocked and heartbroken. We were only a week away from closing the deal with him. A few days after, he stepped out, handing our sale over to his two main employees.

The rest played out in slow motion, like someone else's life. The new guys on our sale had never done an acquisition, and they didn't spend much time with the product before they decided we didn't have enough customers and they didn't like what we had to offer. Three days before closing, our deal was dead in the water.

I was stunned, to say the least. Over the years, I had come to terms with the fact that our product would have to take a different form. But never once had I considered that the project would vanish completely. The project had cost me years of hard work and all my resources, including long hours of my spare time now gone forever. More than once, I had revived it from the dead. I simply did not have it in me to trudge forward with it one more step.

I was kicking myself for choosing the wrong business partner, for disappointing my wife, for investing so much into a project in an industry I didn't fully understand. I had failed completely. I was angry at myself and angry at God—who had, it seemed, left me holding the bag.

To complicate matters, I simply could not imagine going back to my old life as a corporate business consultant. After 20 years on the road, I had found myself with a serious case of microscopic colitis that doctors could not treat. The condition made travel excruciating. This, together with long stretches of time away from family, made me cringe at the thought of taking even one more corporate gig.

Questions crowded my mind. What could I do next? Not surprisingly, my wife was growing more worried every day. How would I support us? How on earth was I going to get out of this mess?

As I ended the call that killed our deal for good, I felt desperate for answers. I stepped into the dining room to deliver the grim news to my wife, who was busy planning her next class. Books on spiritual guidance covered the table.

One jumped out at me. It was Doreen Virtue's book, *Divine Guidance*. Desperate for answers, I followed the tug to pick it up. Without thinking, I flipped through the book—whoosh—until my fingers stopped at a page.

My eyes landed on a section where Doreen encouraged me to ask God a question. First, she instructed, I should slow myself down by taking deep breaths. Then I could ask my question aloud, mentally, or by typing it with a keyboard. The trick, she explained, was to let go of any results and simply wait for an answer.

Well, I had my laptop, and I certainly had a burning question. I had dozens. In that moment, I could not imagine anyone other than God who could answer them.

I sat down with my computer, took three deep breaths, and, key by-key, pecked out a question:

How should I proceed to have a successful career and achieve my purpose?

Then the electricity came. It was not a fluffy-cloud spiritual experience, either. I was completely taken over by the energy, my whole body vibrating. A part of me was terrified.

On the other hand, there was so much love and caring in the experience that I felt held, wrapped in warmth. The language coming through was beautiful, too, nothing like my own voice. I remember thinking, *Who talks this way?* In that moment, I didn't even understand the answers coming. But instead of pushing them away, I allowed them to unfold. While keenly aware that my fingers typed without me, I focused on reading the words as they flowed onto the screen.

Breathe with the intent to calm the mind and soothe the cells of the body. Extinguish the fires of physical inflammation and emotional irritation with the healing waters of a calm mind.

A healthy diet, exercise, quiet relaxation, and meditation will also bring relief, providing a soothing energy to the all-important neurons and synapses in the brain.

In the corporate world you worked with team spirit, and we all were there to support you. You radiated a healing light to all who participated in those teams. Still, the corporate environment didn't allow you to fully express your spiritual self. We are still here to help you in any endeavor you choose, but we hope you choose one that allows your inner light to shine as brightly as it can.

Find the business opportunity in meditation. Meditation itself can be a business. Many seek teaching, encouraging, coaching, and support, which can be very helpful to the initiate. Even advanced meditators who have lagged behind in the other life skills can benefit from coaching.

Therapy is also a useful tool to help achieve self-realization, as well as many other body-mind-spirit practices. Reiki comes to mind. You're good with your hands and very familiar with psychic energy and energetic healing. These are practices that would heal you as you heal others. Your skill in working with groups to heal and inspire them is well-developed, though you have not given yourself the chance to stretch out in the spiritual realm.

The time is now for spreading the word of an ever-increasing vibration of love throughout the world. This is a magical time when all beings can achieve progress on their path to Source.

The veil is thin now between your world and ours. If you wish, you can reach through and provide a conduit for the healing love and light energy to flow into your reality. Of course, you and many others already do this to some extent. All we are saying is this can happen in a big way right now.

There is no need to wait, study, or prepare. You are there already. Or should we say, here? "Here" is already in "there." It's being in the Here that gets you there. Once you're Here, in the present, you're ready.

But enough, already!

I laughed as I watched those words appear on the screen. I thought, *Oh, my God, this is a font of wisdom.* I didn't know if it would ever happen again, and I felt I needed to get as many answers as I could. I asked another question, then another. As each question arose in my mind, an answer would start coming through me before I could even finish typing it. Back and forth, question and answer moved quickly through my fingers.

With whom am I conversing?

We are the Beings of Light and the Soul Guardians.

The Beings of Light are advanced souls whose consciousness permeates multiple dimensions from Source to the fine traces of ethers at the expanding edge of creation. This covers a lot of ground, so to speak. Our light-of-awareness, our consciousness, is not linear, not 3-D, 4-D, or any D, nor is it of any time. Suffice it to say, we channel the creative energy of Source.

The Soul Guardians are those you have already met. They travel in lower frequencies than we do and yet still maintain a high rate of vibration to act as go-betweens with those entities and civilizations on the brink of transformation. You have encountered them many times in your dreams. They provide instruction, guidance, and opportunities for spiritual growth.

In opening to our communication, you are taking a long awaited step toward achieving your purpose. Not that we're rushing you or anything, but you have been capable of this all along. As we said earlier, now is the time to get this going. Your block to writing has made dialogue with us difficult in the past.

Why is this dialogue important?

Transmitting and translating our energies works to clarify and purify your energy as the messenger. It also raises the vibration of everyone it touches by healing the body, enlightening the mind, and inspiring the soul toward spiritual development. Earth needs this now, and so do you, along with everyone on the planet.

The actions you are taking to center and heal yourself create the opening for us to talk with you.

What should I do with this ability?

Sit, write and publish. Spread the word. The main thing is to get started. We will help by guiding you from where you are to where you want to be.

I was like a little kid talking on the phone. I really wanted to keep the Beings of Light and Soul Guardians on the line, but I didn't know what to say next. I reached for a familiar question, what I might ask a new acquaintance at a party.

What do the Beings of Light and the Soul Guardians actually do?

Our point of view is very difficult to put into words. What we do is easy enough to talk about but still can be difficult to understand from a human perspective.

It is our charge to oversee the unfolding and development of consciousness throughout the many galaxies we serve. Since the beginning, life has been unfolding and getting to know itself. The beginning is the first thought, sometimes called the Word or the Uni-verse, the One Word.

We say the beginning "is" instead of "was" because it is still happening Now, with new universes and galaxies forming outside of time as you know it. God the Creator manifests universes in layer after layer of forms and energies, bending time, space, and consciousness in an immeasurable arc of light to which there is no end and no beginning. It is.

Wow, you're right. This is hard to describe, especially since the physics of it are unfamiliar to me.

Spiritual consciousness is more useful than physics to understand your place in God's creation. Awareness unfolds like a hand, opening to receive a seed to be planted and nourished to fruition. Soul Guardians are present as each soul is "born," emerging from Source. We stay at various levels of contact with each entity as its conscious awareness grows.

Since we are all one from Source, how can you be separate from the newly birthed soul?

You could say we are already one with that soul, and you would be correct. However, we also are separate entities with our own missions to complete.

How can the Soul Guardians possibly care for all of those souls?

There could never be too many souls in our care. In fact, that question is a good example of linear thinking. If we are to do this together, your thinking will have to expand.

Then you really are all-powerful?

We are all-powerful from your point of view. But we are completely of service to the souls in our care.

Each soul has a unique frequency and is an individual entity while retaining the totality of Source within it. Unfolding in consciousness is the process of opening to the breathtaking expression of the love and light energy of Source already within you. Full expression is recognizing your singular self, while also living in Oneness with Source. You could say it is like being here and there at the same time. Perfect Oneness can be known, but then, of course, there is no you there to perceive it.

However, you can merge into and emerge from Source at will, just as you have. By practicing that, you come to understand that separation from Source is an illusion.

We are all an expression of the same Self. So learn to express your Self!

2

Full Circle

"We have a deep, loving concern and responsibility
for your development."

~Aion

Everything was happening at once. The words appearing on the screen, the questions lining up in my head, the energy pouring through me and the blur of my body still far away—all of it together reawakened a distant memory.

Years before, in my twenties, I had seen myself as a spiritual seeker. My decision at age 30 to learn to "drink beer, eat meat, and watch football," to focus on business and the practical, down-to-earth side of life, had led me to stash that spiritual version of myself away in the closets of my mind. Now, with this powerful energy coursing through me, that part of me demanded attention.

I was remembering events surrounding my birthday when I turned 35. I had done something very out of character at the time, choosing to celebrate by attending a three-day transformational healing conference. At the end of each day, we listened to a "walk up the mountain" visualization that encouraged us to release anything from the past we no longer needed.

During the meditation at the end of the first day, a powerful energy began pulsing through me. It would hit the crown of my head, then crash down into the base of my spine with a force that sent shock waves through me. I started hyperventilating, trying not to freak out

9

as the intensity grew. As the visualization came to a close, I found that controlling my breath reduced my fear, so I could tolerate the intense energy moving through my body.

A beautiful second day of clearing practices ended in another closing meditation much like the first. As before, energy coursed up and down my spine with tremendous force. Somehow I was able to let it move, in spite of my trepidation. I could feel it blocked at my throat, piling up like a logjam in a river. But I was able to use my hands to move it by swirling them around the area, which seemed to relieve the pressure.

When the same energy came during the meditation on the last day, it had built such momentum around my throat that it did some kind of short circuit. Suddenly I was out of my body, facing a wall of white light.

In a flash of inspiration, I realized that if I increased my frequency, I could pass through the barrier in front of me. So I matched my vibration to the vibration of the field ahead, and—boom—I was on the other side.

It was like breaking through the surface of water. Every molecule of my body exploded in a thousand different directions. I was everywhere and nowhere, completely gone. And then—whoop—I was back again, on the side of the wall of light where I had started, still vibrating. Pulsing with light.

I thought, "Oh my god, I just merged with the light." And then, "I'm gonna do it again!"

I moved toward and then into the wall of light, which was something like a thick, swirling mist of white energy. As I stepped in, I started shifting my vibration to match it, as if making friends with the energy. Fear, the fear of losing myself completely, presented an invisible barrier. I even had the thought that the people around me would find me dead on the floor at the end of the seminar.

"I don't care," I told myself. "I'm going in!"

With this thought, I crossed through the barrier again and dissolved completely. Then, just as before, I popped back to the place where I had started. The experience of being on the other side, completely merged with the light, was more powerful than anything I had ever known.

One more time I tried the experiment, changing my vibration and passing through the field of white energy and my own fear, exploding into nothing, then blinking back into focus where I had begun. Three times I had merged with the light.

As this point, the facilitators of the conference were guiding us to come back from the meditative state, into the room. Perhaps my body was listening to them, because—bam! I was suddenly back in my body. Then back out, then in, my breath carrying me back and forth between the two realms.

I had a friend come lie down on top of me to ground me, which helped stabilize me some. But I couldn't walk, and I was seeing energy everywhere—in the space, in the air, around everyone else. They took a group picture with me propped up on two people, my arms draping over them and a dopey, blissed-out look plastered over my face. In the end, people had to pack up my stuff for me, and somebody drove me home in my car. Two big guys had to help me get in and onto the couch because I could barely walk.

With me on the couch, my wife at the time started taking off my shoes. I warned her to go easy, since I hadn't changed my socks in three days. But as she pulled them off, she started sniffing my feet. I was completely baffled and asked her what in the world she was doing. Then she started sniffing me all over.

"What's going on?" I insisted.

She put the palm of my hand up to my nose.

The smell of incense and roses poured out of me. Out of the soles of both feet, the palms of both hands, and the top of my head, out of the pores of my skin.

"I know this smell," she told me, retrieving a vial of Sai Baba's vibhuti (sacred ash) from the next room. It had the exact same smell.

In bed, I leaned back against the pillows and found myself almost immediately in some other place. I was lying on a cold stone table, very smooth, with someone on my left who seemed to be talking about me. Through a haze of energy, I could hear him saying, "This monad, blah blah blah, monad, blah blah blah, monad, blah blah."

This guy was talking about me, and it was really irking me. I tried to move, but I was completely paralyzed. I couldn't move a muscle. Forget this, I thought forcefully. I'm sitting up.

Using my mind, I brought all that energy from the conference back into my body. Suddenly I was sitting up in the middle of a vast amphitheater filled with people, hundreds of them rising up in steep tiers around me, some like I had never seen before—different skin tones, unusual shapes, big eyes. A lot of them were wearing robes with hoods, up or down, and their attention was focused completely on me.

In the center tier to my right sat a panel of five. They wore elaborate robes draped with sashes in wild, vivid colors, tones I can't really describe because I have never seen them anywhere else. I knew immediately that these guys were the big kahunas.

A hush went over the crowd the moment I sat up, the whole place breathing out a shocked, "Ohhh!" Just then, the "heavy" in the middle of the panel, obviously the leader, stood up. He sliced the air horizontally with his arm, his eyes locked on the person in white next to me who had been speaking. Following the leader's direction, the man next to me now moved his own arm over my body in a similar slicing motion that sent me back against the stone slab and into my body.

Wide awake, I jolted straight up in the bed and turned to my wife.

"What's a monad?" I demanded, stunned. "What's a monad?"

She had been studying Raja yoga, and she pulled down this little blue book called The Monad, all about the indivisible part of a person's soul that makes each of us unique.

For the next three days, my body was shot. I couldn't work and spent my time on the couch or moving my arms, hands, and legs slowly through the air in what seemed like my own version of tai chi. I was doing my best to get back into my body.

Along with being amazed, I felt scared and confused. I had finally crossed a fear barrier that had held me back for years, and I was streaming with energy, seeing light everywhere. But this strange encounter—I couldn't tell if the people in that amphitheater were trying to teach me, heal me, or kill me. I was feeling very uncomfortable, a bit paranoid even, about what had just happened to me. I felt as though beings I did not trust were judging me, with no say in the matter.

The discomfort of that earlier experience had never really left me. But now I found myself engulfed in love, with access to a profound wisdom that was answering any question I asked. I was hungry to know what the Beings of Light and the Soul Guardians had to say about my experience.

At the Transformation Conference in January 1985, I experienced three days of rising kundalini energy, passed through the veil and merged with the light. Afterwards, I dreamed a panel of five beings evaluated me. What was that about?

We were watching over you as your spiritual energy spiked during the exercises at the conference. Your previous energy experiences, combined with your desire to merge with the light, resulted in a short circuit of energy around the block in your throat chakra, precipitating the state of ecstatic bliss in which you found yourself at the end of the conference.

It was the Soul Guardians you saw when you woke up in our "grand rounds," as they would be called in a teaching hospital. That was no dream. It is unusual, but you were so charged with Source energy that you were able to will yourself awake in our plane of consciousness as we discussed your case.

Yes, I was the one who stood up and indicated to your guardian angel to put you back under so we could get on with the discussion. There is nothing to fear in this. We have a deep, loving concern and responsibility for your development.

You were developing faster than you could integrate at that time. We thought it best to slow you down a bit for your own safety. Your nervous system had been burned by previous spontaneous expressions of that energy within you.

I was the guide in the middle of the five. I serve as the master guide on your panel. We have guided you, and countless others, for all time. But it seems like only yesterday when I witnessed your soul first emerge from Source. Over time, let's say eons, souls evolve in consciousness, and roles change according to the needs of the One.

My name is Aion. I'm glad to be having this conversation with you and hope we can continue to bring the joys of transformation to light.

With this, my first transmission from Aion ended. Dazed, I stared at the screen as the energy gradually faded.

As I reread what had appeared on the screen, I felt a host of different emotions. I was both humbled and overwhelmed, amazed to have received such powerful, otherworldly contact. I also felt great relief to know this loving presence, Aion, had been the leader on the council in my earlier experience, and those beings I encountered then had not been out to get me. Instead, these caring beings had been watching over me, not just in this lifetime, but also in those before it. Realizing this brought tears of gratitude to my eyes.

At the same time, the answers I received gave rise to even more questions. Was I in touch with just one being, or many? Who exactly was Aion, and why had he—or was it they—contacted me? Would something like this ever happen to me again?

Still, I found myself in a very elevated state of bliss. The problem with that? I was a corporate guy, boots on the ground and living in the real world. I was a wine connoisseur, not a mystic. Honestly, the Beings of Light, the Soul Guardians, Aion—the whole thing sounded like something out of Harry Potter. Even in that state of amazement, I heard a thought issue from some cynical corner of my mind: What's the big deal?

Actually, it would take months, even years for me to realize the full meaning of the message I had received.

3

All in a Day's Work

"There is nothing like a day for us. All timeframes
are simultaneous, and events happen on
multiple dimensions. But it's all in a day's work!"

~Aion & The Beings of Light

When I woke up the next morning, I was still riding high from my experience the day before. I honestly doubted I would be able to make contact again, but I hoped I could. When I decided to try, I considered it an experiment. If I never heard from these Soul Guardians again, well, I could check the box next to, "Temporarily body-snatched for cosmic purposes," and that would be that.

Sitting down with my computer, I made a little prayer. It went something like, "OK, I don't know how this is supposed to work, but if you want to talk, here I am." Then I typed a question.

Thank you for talking with me. I am most interested in what you do. What is your day like?

And with this question, a feeling of laughter rose up inside of me. I saw the image of a day dawning, then melting away, until I found myself at the center of the cosmos surrounded by stars, plasma, and vivid colors. It was like moving three-dimensionally through the gorgeous pictures I had seen from the Hubble Telescope, the whole of creation unfolding around me. As before, I had the strange ability, despite dyslexia and lack of training, to type like a pro. But instead of being far away, my hands in front of me glowed with a golden light.

I typed:

There is nothing like a day for us.

This was my translation into words of the picture-word-experience I had just received. In my gut, I felt a distinct up-and-down sensation that I took to mean "yes," a confirmation that my words matched the energy of what Aion had transmitted to me.

As I moved through creation, I experienced a sense of being outside of time as I knew it, like being part of many things happening in many dimensions all at once. To explain it, I typed:

All timeframes are simultaneous, and events happen on multiple dimensions.

Again I got a distinct, up-and-down "yes" in my gut.

Visuals and sensations unfurled in me in clear, distinct chunks. In a sudden plop of words, I got:

But it's all in a day's work!

So this new experience of scribing began. Again, I often received answers before I could even fully form questions. The thought came, "How am I contacting you?" But before I could type it, Aion answered:

We are called by conscious intention from anywhere and any when....

If my words failed to capture the intended meaning of the energy coming through, I would get a distinct, back-and-forth "no" hit in my gut, leaving me to try again until I got the "yes" from Aion on what I was writing.

From time to time, I would stop and take a breath, and the internal scene would shift. I did my best to keep up with the energy pictures and word chunks coming through me.

Here is my record, in words, of my 3-D language-picture experience-conversation with Aion.

Thank you for talking with me. I am most interested in what you do. What is your day like?

There is nothing like a day for us. All timeframes are simultaneous, and events happen on multiple dimensions. But it's all in a day's work!

We are called by conscious intention from anywhere and any when. The call may come from a soul wanting energetic release, freedom from a painful physical vibration, or negative emotion. Calls that come from souls with a powerful commitment to heal and elevate their vibration get my immediate attention.

Now you see how the words you choose color the felt experiences I am transmitting to you.

I'm trying to translate but finding it difficult to shoehorn this gigantic, dynamic experience into small words.

Yes, I see you are trying your best, and you are doing a pretty good job. For instance, the connotation of the word "negative" is highly charged. Would it imply that we judge your emotions? We do not.

But you do, and a soul may. That soul may cry out to God to take that emotion away and replace it with relief. We direct God's healing energy toward that soul, sometimes to the degree that the individual can barely tolerate, increasing the soul's rate of vibration to help with release if the soul is ready. There is no judgment, only compassion.

All this is to say the word "negative" brings complications to our explanation. The word "immediate" is another one. Since all this happens at the same time, nothing can happen sooner or later than anything else. Yet we can still frame our experience in the limitations of the concept of a day and talk about it as if it were a linear progression.

How about that for confusing? But that's the way it is.

How do you work with souls?

In what might appear to be chaos to you, there are procedures, order, and structure in the way we guide developing souls. We all agree on a unified approach to our work, and we proceed with loving care for each type of entity we guide.

Earlier I spoke of a progression of roles for each soul as it evolves in consciousness. Souls of all types and levels need attention. Light energy, dark energy, particle, wave, or matter. No matter! We are full-spectrum providers. We can do this because of our extraordinary empathy.

What would it be like if you could remember all your experiences and insights since the moment your soul began? That's what it's like for us. We can empathetically experience all of a soul's joy in living, as well as the struggle to hold on to what gives joy and the suffering that comes from it. We understand the grieving when a soul lets go of that struggle and the rejoicing that issues from being in a higher vibration. Feeling the full expression of that cycle of expanding consciousness gives us perspective. For us, empathy is natural and judgment impossible.

You mentioned individual personalities. What about them?

Personalities play less of a role here than they do on the earth plane, but still, individual expression is everywhere.

Play is important work here. We enjoy passing a ball of golden light from one to another, each fielding it in a unique way, adding to its luster, power, shape, or loving vibration, then sending it on its way. Think of a beach ball passed from person to person in the stands of a stadium.

Each player experiences not just the ball of light but also the very processes, thought-feelings, and healing intentions of each previous player. The playfulness, the loving-kindness and appreciation of each being's contribution bring us all into a higher vibration, just as you are feeling a higher vibration now, simply by imagining it.

Imagining your contribution to the ball of light brings you into the game. As you feel it come to you, what will you add? Might you offer some well wishes to those in need of love? A few ergs of healing energy? The shape of a banana, perhaps? How about the memory of your most beautiful sunset or most glorious moment? You see, your experience adds to the whole and contributes to all of creation.

As my conversation ended, I found myself vibrating with energy and light as I had the day before. This session had been very different than yesterday's, and yet it bore so many similarities. Keeping up with the energies, sensations, and pictures coming through while translating them into words had taken my full concentration as Aion patiently guided me.

To be honest, there was still a strong part of me that saw the whole thing as nothing more than an interesting exercise. My attitude was something like... OK, Stevie Ray McHugh has made contact with the other side. Done. Take that one off the bucket list.

4

Trust the Magic

"You all are the magi in magic."

~ Aion

The day after I experienced and recorded these unusual exchanges, my wife and I left for Sedona. We had planned the trip many months before to attend a large metaphysical convention hosted by Lee Carroll featuring big names like Gregg Braden as well as small booths and breakout teaching sessions from a variety of people. I was attending not as a participant but as a scout. My self-assigned mission was to observe with an eye to developing a business model for my wife.

When we met, my wife had been channeling Jesus, called Sananda in Spirit, for years. Even though I felt uncomfortable with the scene surrounding this practice, I could not deny that powerful energy came through her during these sessions. Sometimes it was so strong that I could not stay awake. As any business consultant worth his salt would, I had been encouraging her to convert this hobby into a business. To that end, I wanted to know, who were the people already doing this work, what kinds of teams had they put together and how had they structured their businesses? In my mind, my wife would share the words of Jesus, and I would serve as her manager, the practical business guy I had spent years becoming.

On our first day at the Sedona convention, we stepped up to the table of a psychic offering readings. As the psychic read me, she spoke in passing of my work as a messenger.

My wife and I looked at each other, chuckling. Yes, I supposed my experiences these last two days had been dramatic. But I certainly was not "a messenger."

The woman looked back at us, unblinking. "You're definitely a messenger. You know that, right? Of course you know that."

I laughed it off. It was fine for my wife to do this New Agey stuff, but I had no intention of getting myself wrapped up in it. I was there on business.

One afternoon, I went to see Lee Carroll channeling Kryon on the main stage. At the beginning of the talk, Kryon said to the room, "For those of you who can see, I'm now going to emit a violet flame from the top of my head." Then this beautiful, very stylized violet flame flared out of the top of his head. Wow! I could see it, and I was feeling the energy of it, too. Even more amazing? It was the same energy I had been feeling as I watched my own fingers type words without me just two days before.

Gradually my encounters at the conference began to work on me. I couldn't relate much to the style of most of its presenters, but I could not deny hearing an echo of my own experience in some of what I found at the event. What was it, though? I had meditated on and off for most of my life, but this was as vivid and real as the conversations I had been having with these—these what? Were they angels, these beings I was talking to, or spirits, or just my own wild imagination?

In the end, I settled on calling my experiences "conversations." I decided that even if I could not name or fully understand it, something was clearly waking up in me. So after a 13-day hiatus, I sat down at my computer and began a new conversation.

How can we humans free ourselves from the cycle of attachment you described?

Well, my young padawan, this is a big and important question.

I laughed a little at this Aion, whomever he was, calling me "padawan," what Obi Wan called his apprentice in the first few *Star Wars* movies. Aion and his crew seemed to have a good sense of humor.

All beings have their own cycles and lessons to advance their consciousness. The cycle of attachment I described is well-known on Earth. Who among you has not experienced the joy and pain of this cycle of life? Attachments come in all shapes and sizes, and all of them can lead to a deeper understanding of consciousness. Souls learn who they truly are by discerning who they are not.

For instance, developing habits leads you to define yourself by them. Identifying yourself by certain behaviors, you might say, "I am a collector, a painter, a mother," or whatever. But no matter how souls define themselves, life sends experiences to show them they are not just that definition they created. They are much, much more.

As before, I experienced myself in the scene of the answer. A vast barn full of thousands of unique and rare artifacts became, in words: "I am a collector;" another image of an artist at his easel was, "a painter," and so forth. As the language for these images downloaded through my brain and fingers, I felt just like an apprentice, a neophyte doing my best to keep up with the vast energy moving through me.

Attaching yourself to an idea of who you are limits your consciousness. It clouds your awareness of being an expansive, timeless soul. Typically, these self-identifications make death something of a shock.

What is death?

The death transition is quite an aha! moment for most beings. Looking back at life from the completed transition, most wonder just how they could have forgotten their spiritual magnificence during that lifetime. From that new vantage point, it is easier to see the cycles of life and their impact over multiple lifetimes.

A question formed in my mind: is reincarnation real? Do we actually live multiple lives? As would continue to happen throughout my experience with Aion, the answer came through before I could type the question.

Yes, most spirits reincarnate again and again, trying to remember who they really are. Most people don't remember past lifetimes because they struggle just to wake up from their identifications in this current life. Experiencing multiple lifetimes allows a soul to expand awareness and grow toward becoming one of us, a luminous being of light, all-compassionate and fully aware.

Why are we so afraid of death?

Death is a translation of identity. It is like a translation from one language that you understand to another that you currently don't. As in spoken languages, the words mean roughly the same, but some subtle and not-so-subtle shifts of perception occur. The seeming loss of self, fear of the unknown, and fear of losing the body and personality with which a person has been so identified creates what we could call separation anxiety.

That fear of separation from the body sends many souls into shock after passing through the veil. But then you find you are still you, only different. The idea of the body persists for as long as the soul needs for comfort and recovery. And more experienced beings are on hand to help souls regain their particular level of awareness in Spirit.

There is no judgment. Each soul has a perfect place to continue on the path to higher realization, and there is much to learn between lives. It is a joyous time of reunion and communion for all.

If life on the other side is so great, why are we here on Earth?

Life on Earth helps a soul make rapid spiritual progress. Experiencing the cycles of life in a conscious way makes the translation easier and even a joyous occasion.

Even for children?

Age at the time of crossing has little to do with how far a soul has progressed. Realization of the truth occurs in no time at all. No one is too young to die. What would be the point of holding a soul back?

Getting back to your original question, to free yourself from the cycle of attachment, practice living in both worlds. Every cycle of attachment, loss, and realization is a little death and rebirth. So practice letting go while you are here on Earth. If you can step back from yourself and let go of your identifications and beliefs for just a brief moment, you can enter into the Here and Now that spans both worlds.

Going inside brings you outside. The micro becomes the macro. Emptiness and fullness disappear. Light and dark are one. You are free to move about the Universe!

With the words "going inside brings you outside," all my energy and attention pulled into my cells until I burst through a membrane of light, into completely empty space that also, paradoxically, felt totally filled with energy and love. An incredible rush of image and experience, almost overwhelming, washed through me as I typed the words.

The energy of this communication struck me deeply. I was buzzing for days, what felt like my whole nervous system rewiring itself. I had the idea to take a year off from work to do nothing but communicate with this being called Aion. But the moment I had that thought, fears around money, business, the house—essentially, all of my identifications—were in my face. Self-doubt flooded me.

It took me five days to work up the courage to sit with my computer again. When I did, I was looking for practical answers to the issues that I had spent so much time thinking about since my last conversation with Aion.

How can I let go and still have goals in my life to create the life I want?

Ah, now there's the rub. You want to hang on to the things, the ideas, the hopes, dreams, and fears you foist upon yourself, all to give yourself a sense of self instead of a connection to your Higher Self.

Please don't take this badly. We are your brothers and sisters in Spirit and are not here to judge. It pains us sometimes, though, to watch the process of your consciousness evolving. And they say that making sausage is hard to watch!

What is the difference between evolution and enlightenment?

Your confusion is due to linear thinking. You assume there is an optimal end state, but no such end state of enlightenment exists.

You do lighten up as your consciousness evolves. As your spiritual awareness grows, the increased light from your energy body illuminates everything around and within you. Increased awareness takes your perception to a higher frequency, providing a more elevated viewpoint from which to know Spirit.

Evolution is the natural progression of a soul toward Source. Enlightenment is but a moment perceived, an aha! experience. Each moment you fully experience brings a flash of enlightenment. Your eyes open a bit more to the true nature of the universe.

In my few moments of enlightenment, merging with the light, I experienced bliss beyond anything I could have imagined. But afterward, I felt kicked out of Heaven.

Your disappointment with those enlightenment experiences is due to the natural return to the moment, which you were trying to avoid.

There is only this moment. It is ignoring the magnificence of this moment that causes your pain and suffering. Embrace this empty moment and leave the rest behind. You can't avoid the void.

To grow in the light of Spirit requires facing the fear of emptiness. It is not true that if you merge with the moment, you will disappear. That's the ego talking, the "you" which perceives through the senses, colored by limiting beliefs of who you are. There is no deep dark void; there is only light. The "dark void" is avoidance, nothing more.

With this, I remembered my own experience of the void. It happened during a time of big and painful changes in my life. I dreamed I was drifting through black space. I felt fearful, small, and alone, as though I had been abandoned by Spirit. With a huge, aching need, I began calling out for God. "I want to see you! Where are you?"

I focused all of my emotion on my desire to see God. "Show yourself!" I demanded.

Suddenly, I was seeing into deep space. My eyes were like a telescope. Spinning, I saw brilliant stars and galaxies all around me. But I wasn't just seeing space; I was in space.

But fear still constricted my chest. I thrashed like a fish on the beach, but I continued calling out.

"God, where are you? I want to see you! Don't leave me in this empty darkness!"

I rotated slowly, the radiant, unblinking stars revolving. I couldn't tell if I was falling at an unimaginable speed or standing still in space. Those impossibly distant sparks of white light amplified the darkness and emptiness.

Adrift, standing on nothing, I screamed, "Please, I want to see you, God!"

A warm and comforting male voice said, "Stevie, stop trying so hard."

I exhaled, released the tension and fear from my body, and softened my vision. Suddenly, the space around me filled with strands of humming energy. Each strand had a core of liquid white light that extended infinitely in a taut, straight stream. Winding bands of golden energy coiled around and around each white core, lending the strands a radiant glow and a deep, resonant tone. I thought of the thick bass strings in a piano, except these strings were innumerable, parallel to and stacked on top each other. An impenetrable blackness that seemed to serve as insulation separated each string.

The strings throbbed sub-sonically, clearly transmitting energy. My heart was bursting with joy.

The voice said, "The empty darkness is full of light. There is simply nothing to be illuminated."

I was astonished. Even though I was drifting through space, I felt held, wrapped in love. My fear disappeared, washed away by the healing vibration emanating from these strings of energy.

Aion, was that voice you?

Yes, you heard me. There's no need to shout. To hear me, simply call, and I will always answer. Then it's up to you to be listening.

This just seems so magical. But I am beginning to believe this is really happening.

There is no magic in us conversing. This is completely normal. It's just ignored or forgotten.

You remember Mr. McGillicuddy, your invisible friend as a child?

Mr. McGillicuddy had been what most adults would call my imaginary friend. And yet, there had been nothing imaginary about him to me.

He had first appeared to me at around age three, wearing an antique suit of thick wool in orange and brown plaid over a white shirt with a narrow, round collar and a string tie. With his ruddy skin, bright blue eyes, and heavy Irish brogue, Mr. McGillicuddy seemed always to be smiling. He was not much bigger than I was at the time, his legs hanging down no more than 18 inches when he sat on a counter next to me. Though I had never heard of or seen one when I met him, "leprechaun" is the best word I can find to describe him now.

Mr. McGillicuddy was always very kind and gentle. In our little preschool band, I played the triangle. But my rhythm was terrible. Thankfully, Mr. McGillicuddy would give me cues for when to hit my notes. After band practice, he would offer me advice. He explained things to me such as how to treat the little girl who was my preschool crush. I would feel his presence over my left shoulder as I pushed her on the tire swing. "Not too high or too fast, now, Stevie," he would say. "You must watch out for her and keep her safe."

I shared many conversations with Mr. McGillicuddy, all focused on manners, friendship, and getting along with others. His insights were just like an adult's.

At Aion's mention of the little Irishman, whom I had completely forgotten about, a rush of fond memories poured through me.

Mr. McGillicuddy is an angelic guardian for children in difficult times. When the two of you talked together about life and love, right and wrong, did it seem magical at the time?

I recall it seeming perfectly natural and very comforting to talk with Mr. Mc-Gillicuddy. So natural, in fact that I kept telling my mother about our conversations, and she assumed Mr. McGillicuddy was a friend of my grandfather. I thought everybody had a small man with an Irish accent to help with problems.

Exactly. Children see the natural and the so-called supernatural as simply their world. This is a viewpoint from which more adults could benefit.

You all are the magi in magic. Each and every soul can work transformational wonders. Simply trust your Higher Self. Trust as a child who sees both worlds as one.

When my mother asked my grandfather about Mr. McGillicuddy, he said he didn't know anyone by that name, and he knew every Irish person in town. After that, my mother told me that it was not nice to make things up and pretend they were true. Essentially, she implied that I was lying. I remember sitting on the kitchen floor under our old wooden table after she said it feeling angry, resentful, and disappointed.

I don't remember seeing Mr. McGillicuddy much after that.

Society, religion, and family all conspire to drive the magic out of children. The genius of a child's insight is too close to an adult's definition of insanity. They strive to keep the genie bottled up, leading to more lifetimes of dissatisfaction, confusion, and repeat performances.

You remember the Bible's reference to the "sins of the father?"

I knew what Aion was referencing and went for a Bible to look it up. I found: "[God] will by no means leave the guilty unpunished, visiting the iniquity of the fathers on the children and on the grandchildren to the third and fourth generations" (Exodus 34:7 NASB).

Aion continued.

The word "iniquity," also often translated "sin," is misleading here; the text actually refers to unconsciousness.

Although parents talk about raising children, much of that conditioning is lowering the child's consciousness to the parent's level. This seems right and proper to parents, inserting the child into his or her place in society, instilling unconsciousness and guilt. Unfortunately, this perpetuates unconsciousness on the planet and leads to acting out in the family.

"The guilty" are only "punished" because their ego and guilt keep them separated from the joy of Spirit in the moment. It looks to them like the wheel of karma or slavery to genetics, but these become an excuse for not transforming now.

I couldn't have said it better myself.

You yourself did say it. There is really only one of us here.

5
Who is Aion?

"I am. I am spaceless space and timeless time."

~ Aion

From Day 1, I had wondered about the being or beings with whom I had made contact. Based on that first experience, it seemed I had connected with a group of energies, the Beings of Light and the Soul Guardians. But I had also been given a name: Aion. Much as I tried, I could not wrap my rational mind around it.

When I shared my experience with other people, they often asked, "Who is Aion?" Many encouraged me to ask Aion directly for more details. People asked, who was this being, where did Aion fit in the cosmic hierarchy, and what was Aion's role in creation?

But I felt shy about bringing these kinds of questions to my conversations. The energy I received from this being was so big and so majestic that I felt dwarfed by it, even intimidated. Asking for intellectual details felt impertinent to me—not to mention the fact that the whole idea of a cosmic hierarchy left me uncomfortable at best. I thought of it as a human concept projected onto the unseen realms.

Originally, I had wanted to focus on connecting with the energy moving through me from these beings without getting too caught up in the metaphysical details of who they were. But eventually even my own curiosity was beginning to get the better of me. With some trepidation, I finally decided to ask.

Aion, can you please explain who you are? Are you an Archangel?

No, I am a father to archangels, a grandfather to angels, and a guide to all souls. Suffice it to say, I am a very old soul, the first consciousness to be "born," or, more accurately, expressed from Source, the Great Central Sun.

Why haven't I heard more about you?

I have had no name and many names. Ra, Brahma, Chronos, and, of course, Aion.

Aion was Ra? I was flabbergasted. I stumbled around for my next question.

What should I call you?

Let's stick with Aion for now.

Aion, you are the Egyptian god Ra? The Sun God?

I am.

I am spaceless space and timeless time. I am pure awareness, one consciousness containing many. I am Oversoul under God.

Ra is just what I was called by a group of souls in Egypt. But I have been guiding souls throughout the multiverse since, well, since time began.

Please don't let these linear thinking phrases distract you from the truth of a-temporality and multi-dimensionality. We could just as easily have said, "forever and ever" or "since consciousness began," but these would be misleading as well.

You can think of me as the first-born "Son" of God.

I thought Jesus was the Son of God.

Yes, we are brothers in Spirit, in service to Source. I have never incarnated. Jesus is the Christed One, and he, through his earthly incarnation and his magnificent leadership in Spirit, has guided all souls a great distance along their path back to the Godhead.

What is your form like?

My frequency, my consciousness spans all dimensions, all time and space. But not every being here in Spirit is expanded to such a degree. There are those who modulate their frequency within a more narrow bandwidth to better serve other dimensions.

You can do this, too. It's a natural part of soul integration. Sending messages, reaching across dimensions, passing through the veil are skills you have and can develop further. It's very much like learning to translate our transmissions as you are doing now. Once you do it, it feels natural and you wonder how you got along without it.

I am deeply honored to be in conversation with you.

And I with you, my son.

This exchange left me in awe. Aion was so much more than I had assumed—a being and a state of being, an individual and a vast consciousness, grander than any I could imagine.

Knowing more about Aion made me feel humble, small. Why would the great sun god, Ra, decide to use my laptop for messages to Earth? And what did he mean by saying he was the firstborn Son of God? Instead of giving me answers, this conversation actually brought more questions. I was intrigued.

Over the weeks and months to come, I began digging into the meaning of the word "aion." Turns out, it is an ancient Greek word for "life" and "flow," often the flow of rivers and time. In Middle English, aion became aeon, then eventually eon, what we think of as a very long period of time. The word aion appears hundreds of times in the Greek version of the Old and New Testaments and was mistakenly translated as "eternal," making damnation to hell forever, rather than for an age or time of separation from God with a beginning and end.

These meanings must have come from the fact that Aion was a Greek god, associated again and again with the cyclical nature of time. The Greeks connected him with the zodiac as the god who witnessed the turning of time's wheel without being affected by it. In Greek art, he most often stood inside of a circle, the classic symbol of timelessness. Later he became the prime Hellenistic diety, the God above all gods in the Greek pantheon.

Eventually people would connect Aion with Chronos, just as Aion had told me in this transmission. Chronos was a god who represented linear time with past, present, and future, from which we derived our Father Time. But the concept of Aion as the being outside the flow of time seemed the most enduring thread in my research. It amazed me to find time figuring so prominently in what I had found, since the nature of timelessness had become a common theme in the transmissions and one that would be developed even more in future conversations.

In all honesty, though, my deeper questions about Aion's identity were not fully satisfied by this inquiry. I had the niggling sense that there was more to Aion than I had even begun to grasp. Aion's reference to being the Son of God had definitely piqued my curiosity. Did he and Jesus, so important both in my Catholic upbringing and my post-Catholic spiritual life, have some kind of direct connection? Whether or not they did, I had a strange, indescribable sense that Aion was, on one hand, vast and unknowable, and yet also a presence that had always been with me.

Perhaps it was this unfathomable mix of mysterious familiarity—or was it familiar mystery?—that strengthened my resolve to continue the conversation I had begun.

6

Modulating Vibration

"Stay tuned to your highest frequencies and
let us guide you."

~Aion

As I opened more to the multi-dimensional messages I was receiving from Aion and the Beings of Light, my life began to transform. I was thrumming with energy in a way I hadn't in years, even when I was not receiving messages from Aion. Colors became more vivid, my experience of the natural world more engaging than ever. I could stand before the spring blossoms on a lilac bush and literally see a gorgeous energy pulsing through the branch and bud. I felt an underlying connection between that energy and my own, as if everything around me was filled with the same juice, all of it moving out from a single, shared heartbeat.

The more I experienced this expansion, the more I wanted to live in it all the time. Often Aion's downloads came with practical guidance on how I could expand even more into the energy I was experiencing. But the messages also challenged me, since I had to stretch beyond my current capacity, beliefs, and habits to put their guidance into action. Could I pass through the veil again but stay conscious and connected to this exquisite energy? Could I follow Aion's advice and do what it would take to truly live in both worlds?

Aion, what exactly is the veil?

Think of the veil as a winding ribbon of energy, barely present, that separates earth consciousness from Spirit consciousness. It is so thin that it barely exists at this point. Still, it is there, and it forces a shift in frequency for anything that passes through it.

You might think of it as an energy transducer, a frequency modulator between levels of consciousness. It takes extra energy, an extra effort to pass through the veil and remain conscious.

Right now, we are sending thought packets through the veil by charging them with extra energy. You can then receive them and bring them into form, into words that humans can understand.

When you get stuck or lose focus, take three deep breaths, pause, and begin again. Simple, isn't it?

Yes, it is simple, but complex, too. What do I do once I'm on the other side of the veil?

Open yourself to the love and the energy. Go where you are called. Match your frequency to the caller. Enter into that level and do some good. You will know what to do when you get there. You are a guide, amongst other abilities and responsibilities. There is much to be done, and it doesn't matter where you start.

What other insights do you have for me?

Stevie, you can't live on both sides of the veil without embracing them equally. Trying to squeak by with lip service to Spirit and half-hearted efforts to meditate won't help you bridge dimensions.

Words are not The Word. Actions speak louder than words, but your thoughts are more powerful than both. Thought vibrates at a rate that is closer to the Spirit realm than any other activity on Earth. High vibrational thoughts can bring you deeply into the light and into God's loving arms.

But thoughts lead to physical actions. Is that helpful for evolving the soul?

It is true that thoughts lead to actions. To lead a life of right action, you must regulate your thoughts.

But there is even more to be done with your thoughts and feelings to achieve right vibration, to elevate yourself into the Spirit world while maintaining consciousness on Earth.

Why is living on both sides important?

All souls exist to grow to the next level of awareness. The skill of vibration modulation is paramount for a soul guide.

Imagine being able to increase your frequency such that you can see both the physical and the spiritual dimensions simultaneously. This is a greater freedom. It allows you to remain conscious and travel out of the body to receive lessons and inspiration, as well as to give assistance to souls in other realities.

Those realities are just as real as the one you consciously live in now. You just haven't yet developed the vibration modulation skills to stay conscious in those dimensions. Just as you became aware in our grand rounds, you can wake up in other realities by modulating your vibration.

We in Spirit do this naturally, unencumbered as we are by physical bodies. But that is only the beginning. We must be able to match frequencies with all types of beings, levels of consciousness, and planes of reality. Otherwise, we could not be as helpful for those seeking guidance to merge with the light.

Modulating your vibration means being able to consciously arrive in any dimension and merge compassionately, in total empathy with another soul's reality. I am using the words dimensions, levels, and realities synonymously to describe specific frequencies of consciousness, light, and matter, which exist beyond your current perceptions. These dimensions are inhabited by souls on missions not dissimilar to yours, souls in need of support and encouragement.

You have an expanding role as a guide for souls seeking enlightenment, regardless of which side of the veil they inhabit. To contribute the most, master your ability to modulate your frequency and raise your vibration as well as the vibration of those around you in need of a lift.

Are you describing raising the kundalini?

In part. With kundalini energy, you can leave your body and pass through the veil at will. This you have done before. Don't be afraid; we are here to assist you in passing over consciously. It's good practice for dying and for living consciously.

But there's more to modulating your vibration than just kundalini. That energy is a specific release or burst designed to open the cellular and etheric pathways of the body. Once the pathways are cleared of blockages, all manner of Spirit energy can circulate.

Frequency Modulation Exercise

The key is to modulate the energy. Breathe into it. Change the wavelength. Shorter, faster, higher frequency vibrations that emanate from your body will bring you to the veil. Smooth the vibrations out and speed them up to a higher frequency that moves outward. It becomes more like a hum at the frequency of OM. That is the takeoff point where your body stays here and your consciousness goes there, which is here for us.

Don't worry. We are here to receive you. You can do this as often as you like. There is no damage or harm to you, except, perhaps, to your preconceptions.

Once the chakras within and around the body unify, they light up and pulsate with energy, allowing the soul to vibrate at a much higher frequency. The chakras unify when each chakra is clear of resistance and operates harmoniously with the others, so that it can cycle its specific frequency into the flow of the soul's energy. The flow of energy up the chakras, then down, around, and radiating out in all directions creates a unified field and allows you to change levels of vibration at will.

You have accomplished this. Now is the time to put it to good use by helping others. Help them discover their own ability to change their state at will. They will release pain and gain joy. They will heal their energy leaks and grow in their spiritual capabilities.

What leaks do you mean?

Hopes and fears. Dreams and memories. I must, I want, I can, and I can't. These are all energy leaks, draining attention away from the moment.

I'm surprised you say dreams, hopes, and an "I can" attitude are leaks.

Well, take a deep breath and think about it. A future orientation is just as out of the moment as one focused on the past. The future focus is a bias of yours. Yes, it can help you evolve and grow, but only by fits and starts because it still ignores the present.

But I thought we could create our future by envisioning it, willing it to come to pass.

You are still creating the future by living in the moment.
In your linear world, it looks like one moment leads to the next, but in fact any moment connects to unlimited moments in other timelines and dimensions. These are alternate paths that are open for your exploration and edification. Why limit yourself to a single future vision when there are innumerable ones?

If the futures are already available, then we are not creating them, right?

Let me be more precise. Everything already exists in potential on some level of reality that we, on our side of the veil, are able to perceive. But it doesn't become a reality to which you can relate until you can perceive it.
Consciousness converts a potential into a new reality. It is real because you make it so. You are creating the future by being aware, perceiving a new Now, in the moment. Physicists are correct when they say that viewing an interaction of particles changes their reactions. This is the law of creation.

How can we stay in the moment but still create a successful life? If I do nothing and just experience the Now, how do I live, get a job and raise a family? Don't I need to take action?

There is no conflict here. Actions arise out of the moment. Conscious perception is an action. It creates movement, change, and interaction. This is presence in action, the way of life unfolding.

You are a perceiving entity. You can't help but create. Your life is but a moment. You think you are born, grow up, grow old, and die, and so you do. But you remember your birth perceptions and your childhood thoughts and curiosity. You even remember snippets of past lives. You know you are the same being now as then, a little wiser, perhaps, but the same soul, nonetheless.

Your thoughts create your reality on many levels simultaneously. All of your remembrances and perceptions are available to you, regardless of the time orientation. Look at them as a collage of resources available to help you move from one reality to another at will.

I ask you, how much did attempting to craft any of those lifetimes by willing the future into the present accelerate your spiritual development?

I don't think I know the answer to that.

Well, you do.

OK, I'd guess not much.

And you would be correct. You know for sure because you're back in the body again; same consciousness, different body, repeating the same lessons over again. A soul's consciousness is capable of so much more.

Ouch.

There is no judgment meant or implied. It's just a statement of fact. The Hindus talk about getting off the karmic wheel of life, death, and rebirth, and in that, they are correct. All souls can pass through that stage. But it can happen at any time. There is no law of karma other than what you create.

So I am a soul in training. How do I proceed with that in the moment?

Intend to. It's as simple as that.

Keep the conversation present. Keep learning in the moment. Pay attention to your inner life, in balance with the outer one. Live both simultaneously. Stay tuned to your highest frequencies, and let us guide you. Fear not.

Accept what is Now, and let go of the past and the future. There is no doing to create the future or get the past undone. You control the horizontal, and you control the vertical. Accept who you are in your full, magnificent beingness, Here and Now.

Yes, I will. I do.

That's it! You are on your way to I Am.

7
Lightrider

"Be the beacon. Be your radiant Higher Self, and
you will have achieved your purpose,
Lightrider."

~ Aion

In the very first download from Aion, I had received the guidance, "Breathe with the intent to calm the mind and soothe the cells of the body. Extinguish the fires of physical inflammation and emotional irritation with the healing waters of a calm mind."

At the time, I hardly understood what the words meant. But just three weeks after that very first encounter, I found myself in the midst of a full-blown miracle involving my health.

As I mentioned previously, I had suffered microscopic colitis that doctors considered untreatable. For more than 16 years, I had found myself crippled by debilitating bouts of diarrhea and pain that made my proximity to a bathroom one of the most important things I needed to manage in any given moment.

I had tried everything—prescriptions, supplements, gluten-free, sugar-free, taste-free diets. Some things seemed to work for a few weeks, but in the end, nothing really helped. The condition had escalated to the point that if I wanted to take a 15 minute walk to the coffee shop, I had to do it in a zig-zag route from one construction site's port-a-potty to the next.

Imagine my surprise to find myself free from symptoms after just three weeks of receiving energy downloads from Aion. No more gut pain or bouts of diarrhea, no more obsessive searching for bathrooms. Of course, after so many attempts to change the condition with only temporary results, I was hesitant to really trust it had truly healed.

But now, at six weeks in, I found myself feeling better and better. Light filled my body and mind as I practiced modulating my frequency. The more I experienced the loving vibration of Aion's transmissions, the more I began to understand that my physical healing was directly connected with this work. Tentatively at first, and then with more conviction, I was coming to accept that the changes in my health were lasting. I was normal after 16 years of struggle.

On a deeper level, I sensed this physical healing pointed to something even bigger for me. I was beginning to see that I would never be the same.

A lot of internal changes seem to be arriving. My kundalini energy is moving again and expanding throughout my body. I am experiencing more serendipity, even having a connection with my mother-in-law's thoughts! Can you explain what is happening to me?

Welcome back to the multiverse, the real world, my son. So you continue to awaken. That's good.

Are you feeling OK?

I'm fine, thanks, just a bit confused. I'm excited but wondering how I can make best use of these changes in my energy. I feel like I'm running out of time to complete my purpose in this lifetime.

You have all the time you need, especially as there is no time! These awakenings are a sign that you are on your path. Welcome them and the shifts they bring.

You may find yourself sleeping more or less, with more energy for some activities and less for others. Yes, this energy moving through you changes your motivation, which may require some adjustments in your lifestyle.

Think less and meditate more. Trust even more in your intuition, your knowingness. Yes, there are psychic moments coming through more often now. Let go of belief and disbelief. Learn to simply notice them and trust them. Stay conscious and curious. You can always ask me what to make of any vision, just as you are doing now.

What other adjustments?

Let go of the news and your addiction to it.

This advice shocked me. My involvement with election politics had led to a habit of watching four hours of news a day, something I considered a civic duty. I certainly never considered it could be an addiction. But in the months ahead, I would come to realize how much watching the news lowered my vibration.

Write rather than read. Exercise every day, at least once, sometimes twice. Eat more fruits and vegetables.

Do I sound like your mother yet? Seriously, her advice was always good. Stay hydrated and stay high.

What?

Keep your thoughts and heart vibration on the high side. Staying connected to Spirit leads to faster, smoother advancement, though you will still have to pass through some sticky wickets on the way to higher consciousness.

How can I get unstuck?

Letting go gets you unstuck. It allows Spirit energy to pass through you more quickly, raising your vibration until it is time to let go of your next energy block. We're talking about letting go of attachments, preoccupation with yourself, and your so-called needs.

Ask yourself, what do I really need? We are not talking about wants, here.

When I strip my wants away, all I really need is my next breath.

That's right, as long as we are talking about life in the body.

While you have a body, you'd best use it to advance as far as you can. You can use your breath as a vehicle to unify your field and cross the bridge to the other side. I don't mean just in dying, but also in living.

You are a lightrider, a conduit for energy that spans your world's consciousness and the expanded consciousness of Spirit.

Practice for Passing Through the Veil

See yourself straddling the veil, with one side of you in the waking world and the other in the awakened multiverse.

Suddenly, I found myself transported to a thin ribbon of white light, which I recognized as the veil. A powerful surge of energy shot up my spine, radiating through me. It felt something like putting my finger in a wall socket, electricity zinging through every cell. I moved forward, one half of me remaining in the familiar frequency of Earth, the other half crossing through the veil and into the cosmos.

Feel the energy rise in your spinal column. Radiate this energy from Spirit to everyone and everything on Earth.

Lit up with energy, I turned to look back at Earth as if from space. Without effort, I felt an unspeakable love radiating through me. I sensed that this love was impacting the whole planet and all living things on it. Clearly the love that Spirit holds for all of us now poured through me. My small personality disappeared in this moment of ecstasy.

Now broadcast the collective feelings of your world back to Spirit.

With this instruction, I was no longer myself. Rather, I became the heart's call of every being on Earth. Every wish for healing, guidance, growth, or help became, for an instant, my own. In a surge of energy almost too much for me to bear, all the pain and all the joy of every soul on Earth pulsed through me. As I received these messages, I beamed them from my heart to Spirit through the veil.

Celebrate love.

Love continued to stream through me.

Let the resonance build until you are vibrating in synch with the pulsation of the multiverse. Radiate this pulse from your heart and from all your chakras. Your radiation is the message.

The majesty and wonder I felt at the sight of this stunning planet I called home truly defied description. Gracefully, Aion responded to my wordless state.

This transmission needs no translation. You can speak about it to inspire, you can touch people to heal, and you can simply breathe to raise their frequency. But actually, none of that is required.

Radiate beams of love from your light body. Be the beacon. Be your radiant Higher Self, and you will have achieved your purpose, Lightrider.

The incredible experience still reverberating through me, I fumbled for my next words.

How do I even begin?

Learning to modulate energy is like learning to sing. Singers practice by singing scales. Practice strengthens the vocal cords and expands the range of frequencies the singer can convey.

Think of practicing energy modulation as finding your celestial voice. You have called Spirit to you many times with your natural voice. Now learn to use your supernatural voice.

Yes, you have a throat chakra for singing in your world, but you have so many more chakras that are your instruments for modulation. Each chakra can be activated by a unique frequency and, once activated, can emanate a unique, powerful, and resonant energy, affecting circles within circles of thought, matter, and energy throughout the multiverse.

A single radiant being can fill the so-called void with sound and light. Then every spark of consciousness radiates more brilliantly. Such a celestial song raises all frequencies.

What do I need to do to achieve this?

Awaken your energy centers and unify your energy field. We are helping you, even as you write this, to expand your range of frequencies.

Today when you picked up on your mother-in-law's thoughts, you were on the mother-in-law frequency. Isn't that amazing? When you went to the grocery store and thought to buy watermelon for her, you were on her wavelength.

We can speak in terms of light, sound, or simply of frequency, but understand, to us, it is all the same. Energy is all there is. Whether it is subatomic or supernova, it is the same fundamental energy. And I do mean fun! And mental.

8

Soul Pilot

"By imagining your destination, you arrive there."

~ Aion

Aion, I don't understand how to be in the moment and still hold a compelling vision for an outcome in the future. Can you please clarify?

Ah, the linearity has you again, my boy. Simply imagine the future already existing in the present.
Remember your Soul Pilot dream?

In my late thirties, I had been having trouble sleeping. In my dreams during that time, a woman was teaching me in lectures and conversations that I could not remember when I woke. This woman got louder and louder as time went on, as if trying to get through to me. Instead of making headway with me, though, she simply kept me from deep sleep. Most nights, I responded to the woman by talking in my sleep, keeping my girlfriend awake, too.

To help me, my girlfriend began using hypnotherapy techniques I taught her. By giving me prompts and suggestions to describe my experiences from the state between sleeping and waking, she could follow my experience and influence it. Gradually I began to recall some of these nighttime adventures.

Perhaps the most memorable of these was what I call the Soul Pilot dream. In it, I found myself driving a sleek craft through the black of outer space. In front of me, a huge wraparound windshield offered an incredible view of the stars, overlaid with a heads-up navigational map of that sector of the universe.

My passengers were a ghostly grey old couple who had just died in a car accident when the man had suffered a heart attack and hit a tree. The two were conscious but in shock, neither of them very responsive. My task was to transport them to a place of soul rest and recuperation in a spiral galaxy illustrated on the screen.

En route, I brought our vehicle to a small planetoid I had visited before for a routine pit stop. Using my thoughts, I gracefully brought the vessel in for a landing. As we touched down, I let go of the idea of the ship, and it disappeared. The three of us stood before the thick wooden doors of the gate of a tall log fence, which surrounded an American Southwest desert-style monastery.

The doors of the gate opened, and two nuns in full habit stepped out to greet and escort us into their monastery. One took my charges in each arm, leading them slowly through the gate. The other, who knew my name, informed me that the Mother Superior wanted to see me.

Anyone who attended Catholic schools knows that being summoned by the Mother Superior is usually not a happy occasion. Nervously I followed the nun down a central dirt pathway toward the Mother Superior, who was walking toward me with a large white box in her arms. When she spoke, it was with softness.

"We've been expecting you," the Mother Superior told me. "Your mother left this gift for you," she explained, gesturing toward the box.

"My mother? Is she here?" My heart began to race. At the age of 16, I lost my mother, who had been my best friend. She died in open-heart surgery, and the tragedy left our family in a state of shock and confusion that would shape my destiny. Since her passing, I had never seen nor heard from my mother again, in dreams or otherwise, despite my longing for her. To hear the Mother Superior speak of Mom left me choked up.

"No, she is no longer with us." the Mother Superior answered. "She died from this place before she could finish her studies as a Soul Pilot. But she left this gift for you."

The Mother handed me the box, which I took from her wordlessly.

I carried the box up a flight of stairs, into a small apartment that was mine any time I visited this place. It had a large deck surrounded by a wrought iron railing, mission style wooden deck furniture, and a view of the planetoid's nearby horizon. I sat with the box in my lap, feeling its weight.

My girlfriend, who was awake, had been prompting me to describe what was happening in the dream. Now she intervened. "Open the box," she said to me.

"I can't open the box," I told her from my dream state. Conflicting emotions—excitement at finally having contact from my mother again, fear of what the box might contain, old, unexpressed grief over her death—all churned within me.

"Open the box," she insisted.

I looked at the lid of the box. "There's an envelope," I told her, describing a card-shaped envelope attached to the box.

My girlfriend prompted, "Open the envelope."

"I can't open the envelope," I told her. Instead, I pulled it loose and pressed it to my forehead. As I did, a holographic image of my mother's head and shoulders appeared in front of me.

Standing beside her casket as a teenager at the wake, I had tried my very best to memorize my mother's face. She had been beautiful, just turning 40. But I had failed at keeping that face alive in my mind's eye. This three-dimensional image, while not the same as having her with me, truly captured her essence.

The image spoke.

"I am so sorry I had to leave early, Stevie," she sighed. "I loved you and your sisters so much, but I couldn't finish my mission there on Earth. It was too much for me, and I just had to go."

Tears welled up in my eyes.

"I'm leaving you this gift," she said, as I began to sob. "It will help you in your studies as a Soul Pilot."

With this, her image faded. I reached for my face, trying to wipe it dry. A Soul Pilot? What was she talking about?

I took the top off of the box. Inside was an oversized, leather-bound book, its cover embossed with elaborate symbols in vivid reds, greens, and purples. Some reminded me of star constellations. A wide leather strap stretched from the book's back cover to its front, holding closed 4 inches of pages edged in gold leaf. The strap ended in a large bronze clasp that still bore hammer marks from its forging.

I ran my hand over the cover and lifted the book from the box. Gingerly, I placed it in my lap.

"Open the book," my girlfriend whispered to me from the other side of my dream.

I took a deep breath, looking up at the stars above me. With an exhale, I looked down again at the book and opened its cover.

Some of its pages seemed to stick together. I opened the book there, to a perfect, three-dimensional copy of the heavens above me.

In a flash of inspiration, I took another deep breath and thought of the destination in the spiral galaxy where I would be taking the couple in my ship. I rifled through the pages of the book until my thumb found what felt like a second stopping point. As I opened the book to this new spot, I kept one hand sandwiched between the pages where I had found the first map. From this new section of the book arose another three-dimensional map of the exact place where the couple and I were headed.

Somehow I knew what to do. Holding the pages of the book between these two maps in my right hand, I reached with my left to touch the first map of the stars above me. Instead of resting on that page, however, my hand, then my whole left arm went straight through the clump of pages between the two maps, appearing in the second map of the spiral galaxy, as though I had put my hand through a tube and not a solid book.

Then I understood. This was an interactive atlas, something like a multi-dimensional, intergalactic GPS device.

When I woke, I remembered the dream vividly. Maybe it should not have surprised me that Aion brought it up.

In that experience, your mother gave you a book, an atlas of celestial maps to help you transport newly deceased humans to their rest and recovery planets. You learned that simply by visualizing the stars at the end of the journey, you could arrive there instantly.

Can you see how you simultaneously held the image of the location you were in and the vision of the journey's end? In no time at all, beyond time and space, you arrived at your destination and delivered your charges.

This is non-linearity. Did you actually move through space, or did you just change your perspective?

This is hard to think about, Aion.

It is the thinking that makes it hard. Try simply knowing it, trusting what you already know on a spiritual level.

It is this sixth sense of knowing that enables a soul to bring forward many lifetimes of knowledge and understanding. The sense of knowing makes that which you imagine come to pass. Doubt, especially self-doubt, weakens the ability to manifest.

Are you saying that I didn't actually pilot the ship to the new location, but instead, I imagined the arrival destination, and it came into being because I imagined it so?

Now you are getting closer to understanding. Because you imagined your destination, you arrived in that plane of reality. This is how transportation and manifestation work on our side of the veil. The corollary on your side is similar but happens more slowly, since viewed from the perspective of time.

Similar? How?

Similar in that you hold the image of the current reality and the vision of the end state simultaneously, knowing that it is so. This sets your consciousness in motion and starts you vibrating at the correct frequency for your soul to emerge in that end state.

As you stay focused on that frequency, all of your guides and angels, together with all of your many selves and soul fragments, align to help bring your full consciousness into that reality. This is a lot of help!

A soul can more easily manifest a change in consciousness than, say, turn water into wine. But many so-called problems like aging, disease, material limitations—things that seem solid and unchangeable to you—can be shifted for you to arrive more quickly at your chosen reality. More quickly, that is, from your perspective.

So you're saying that if I want to change a habit, clear a neurotic thought pattern, or transmit your messages out loud, these are things I can easily manifest?

Certainly. You can also work in concert with divine beings to influence the flow of events on the earth plane. As your control of your frequency grows, so do your powers of manifestation. Practice helps build your capabilities as the creator of your reality.

We have talked about radiating love as the most powerful force of change. Acting out of love impacts everyone and everything, including that which you want to manifest. Love accelerates manifestation.

Was that the astral plane I was on during the dream?

Yes, it is a transitional plane that all beings who die experience. There are all kinds of issues and experiences happening on that plane, which makes it a good place for you to train in modulating frequency and maintaining emotional stability.

This challenge is one you are up to, and it can speed your soul integration. Don't worry or be concerned about not knowing exactly what to do. Trust your Higher Self. You can't make any mistakes on that level. It is an act of compassion to help those in need move on to their next resting place. Just being there for these souls is a blessing for them, and it's good for you, too.

OK, let's make this practical. I want to lose weight and regain my skinny self. How do I proceed?

Body-Spirit Connection Exercise

What do you know in your soul that you must change to arrive at your desired, thinner end state?

Beyond the practical stuff of dieting and exercise, I imagine I need to change my frequency most of all.

Yes! Talk to me about that frequency shift.

In that new frequency, I vibrate more deeply, resonating with my connection to Spirit. I tune my vibration to that connection before I put anything into my mouth to see if the food resonates with me. I breathe from my diaphragm, directly into my solar plexus at the third chakra, centering, clearing and grounding. I feel less anxiety and more trust in the flow of my life. I know I am succeeding right now because I am vibrating in the frequency of my skinny self, meaning that I am embodying that self Here and Now.

Name the new frequency.

Ok, I'll call it the Body-Spirit Connection frequency.

Experience your Body-Spirit Connection now. Let the energy of that Spirit connection flow down your spine from the top of your head, through your forehead, throat, heart, and into your belly.

Breathe it into your belly. Feel your belly soften, the energy swirling clockwise, gently dissolving any resistances, blockages, or doubts there. Any dissolved residues simply spin out of your body, out of your field, and harmlessly out into the divine stream of consciousness, where they are washed back to Source.

Currents of refreshing, cleansing energy continue to wash through you with every breath. Wave upon wave of loving energy flows from your head to your belly, relaxing the belly, slowly spinning in the belly, washing away any knots, any fears of lack with the certainty of complete satisfaction. Like wisps of smoke, that which is not your true self spins away into the ethers.

Take another deep breath. Let the loving energy of Spirit wash down upon you, down to your belly, below the belly to the sacral area below the navel, down to the base of your spine, and then to your feet. Let the energy flow beyond your feet, into the earth.

Breathe again, feeling Spirit energy move once again from your head, to your feet, into the earth. Breathe and be a conduit for bringing Spirit energy to the earth plane.

What do you know now?

I know that I am fed, nourished, and satisfied by my connection to Spirit. I know that Spirit energy is my sustenance. I know that vibrating in my Body-Spirit Connection will guide me back to my skinny self.

How's that for practical?

Thank you so much for this experience, the insight and connection.

You're welcome. There is no need to mention it, as we are already One and it is already done.

9

Let Go and Go Deeper

*"The pathway to the truth is broad. It is open
to as many interpretations as there are
souls perceiving it."*

~Aion

One of the reoccurring themes in my conversations with Aion was my own hesitation and doubt about my ability to properly translate the transmissions, especially as I considered sharing them with other people. Aion always addressed these doubts with patience, encouraging me to trust myself—a lesson I had apparently been returning to for a very long time.

Aion, I'm troubled that I won't get the message you are transmitting right. I fear mistranslating your felt images that are so rich, majestic, and meaningful. My inclination is to go back, rethink, and rewrite in an attempt to perfect it. Is this approach appropriate?

Certainly. The transmissions to you are meant for you as a unique soul with your own background and perceptions. The pathway to the truth is broad. It is open to as many interpretations as there are souls perceiving it. Your frequency adds your flavor and color to the transmission.

Still, these messages are appropriate for any willing to hear. They must be taken with a grain of salt, though, since they come through the filter of your personality. Those reading can take what resonates with them and leave the rest.

How can I know I'm getting the message essentially correct?

You know it as it appears, don't you? You know it the instant you perceive it. Why question your knowingness?

Good question. My head questions my heart. Actually, it is more my gut feeling that I question.

Your gut gives you grief when you are off track, doesn't it? It also gives you comfort when you are on a path that resonates with your purpose.

You have lots of guidance from us on the other side. Among other methods, we introduce information directly into your chakras for your processing and guidance. This is why working with your energy centers every day leads to a smoother journey on your path.

Trust your seven senses and the messages they deliver as we work with you.

Receiving these words from Aion jogged my memory. I immediately thought of the sacred journey I took back in 1979.

At age 29, I had found myself at a crossroads. I had made the decision to step away from the spiritual community I knew so well because I felt that I had come to see spiritual practice as a reason to feel superior to other people who were not doing spiritual practice and separate myself from them. As I mentioned before, when I decided to step away from spiritual practice, I made a big deal about how I was going to learn to eat meat, drink beer, and watch football.

But the truth was, I felt lost inside. I no longer considered myself a student of Guru Maharaji, who had been my North Star, spiritually speaking. Without him, I felt disconnected from Spirit. I also felt disconnected from social support, since stepping away from the guru meant leaving the familiar territory of my community. I had no idea how to navigate the world beyond the protective circle I had lived in for 10 years.

In Febrary 1979, I decided to take a medicine journey, an experiment to contact my own guidance and inspiration.

As my body went to sleep, I remained fully conscious. Asleep and awake at the same time! I couldn't help but exclaim at how remarkable it felt. From behind me, a strong but kind arm wrapped around my own chest and arms to help anchor my awareness in this new state.

As I stabilized, a flowing form appeared at the edges of my vision, brushing over one shoulder like billowing pink and purple silk. When I turned to look at her, she had already slipped behind me to my other shoulder. I turned toward her once more, but she swiftly disappeared again around a corner and out of view. Even though I caught only a glimpse, I sensed a deep, soulful quality in this attractive feminine presence.

"Follow me," the voice called to me in lilting tones. Her words were tinged with delight, and she moved like wind along a winding tunnel that glowed as if alive.

Even though I was surrounded by light, I felt myself contract in fear, overwhelmed by the power of this new experience.

"Let go," she said, "and go deeper. Follow me."

With these words, the fear charged through me and melted away, leaving me empty. The silken form swished past again, currents of her airy laughter trailing behind as she led me to the tunnel. She sailed into it, then arched into a dive down its endless length.

"Followw meee... " she called again, her voice echoing up the shaft back to me.

I felt queasy, a fear of heights washing through my gut. Then—gulp—I jumped in behind her, screaming as I fell down the shaft.

Soon falling became something more like flying, my body in a state of suspended animation that made it hard to tell if I was moving or floating in place with the shaft itself whirring past. As if I was in a very fast elevator dropping through floors, scenes whooshed by me in layers, 360-degree images from each one surrounding me as I fell through them.

A green level I saw just below caught my attention. Instantly I was pulled into it, a jungle scene, with rice paddies and villages. Women in straw hats pushed bright green plants into the muddy fields as children played nearby. But the peaceful scene shifted suddenly to chaos as the sound of airplanes filled the sky overhead. I looked up, and the fear of the people in the scene hit me—bam!—like a wave of pain. I watched people begin running out of the rice paddies to their straw-roofed huts, the women gathering children that cried and screamed for mommy.

Their suffering became so overwhelming that I could barely walk or even move. When rockets started raining down, I saw a pre-teen girl get hit. It was napalm. She screamed in agony, her skin melting off her body. As her body burned, so did mine. With no barriers, I felt her shock, confusion, the extreme pain, and under that, some kind of solid, aware core.

It was too much for me to bear. "All right," I declared, "I'm waking up."

As soon as I had the thought, I was back in my body. While it was asleep, I was fully awake but in shock from the girl's experience.

"Wake up, body," I told myself. "Wake up!"

My body stirred, just beginning to respond. But before I could fully rouse myself, I felt a male presence behind me. He wrapped his arm around my chest as he had in the beginning, the way a lifeguard would rescue a swimmer from the ocean. His presence was crystal clear. I found myself staring down at the golden blond hairs on his radiant porcelain skin. An energy of calm poured into and soothed me.

"Let go and go deeper," he said, his voice full of love. "You're only perceiving these things with your seven senses. Put your body back to sleep and follow."

With this, my physical body let out a deep sigh of contentment and dropped off to sleep again.

Through blackness, the shaft opened up before me as before, and I found myself falling through it again. My female guide was down below me, her pink and purple swirl of silk calling to me. By now I understood: Where I put my attention in this realm was where I would go.

Levels opened up around me again as I fell through the shaft. Just below, a pastoral scene appeared. Large granite rock formations rose from one side of a green, grassy valley. The rocky area featured a vast outdoor amphitheater, built not for an audience, but rather for the orchestra gathering there. Smaller stages dotted the hillsides around it, people streaming into the valley from every direction. Some carried instruments, some wore choir robes, and all clustered into groups—pairs, trios, quartets, knots of 10 or 15. Each group formed as if guided by a magnetic, unspoken knowing.

That looks really beautiful, I thought. In an instant, I found myself standing on perfectly manicured grass in front of the amphitheater.

"Ah, you're just in time," a woman greeted me. I looked at her quizzically. "It's the convocation to Spirit we do every evening at sunset. Would you like to join us?"

Even without a path, my feet knew where to take me. A tug in my chest drew me to a gorgeous old oak tree, at least 4 feet in diameter. Three others approached as I stood beneath it, one carrying a bass, another, a violin, the third, a viola.

The trio smiled at me, opening their cases and preparing their instruments without speaking. I stood there awkwardly, wondering what I should do. The woman with the violin sent me the thought, "Oh, you're the cello."

"But I didn't bring an instrument," I thought back to her.

In her mind, she laughed. "What do you mean? You are the cello."

I looked down. In my hands, a cello's voluptuous brown shape appeared.

"What? But I don't know how to play the cello."

She only laughed again. From the amphitheater I heard the tap, tap, tap of a conductor's baton. The whole place went silent.

But in a flash, music was everywhere. The random notes of musicians tuning their instruments I had heard upon entering the scene now blossomed into a glorious symphony around me, the music of an inspired composer that I felt somehow I knew. The voices of choirs blended together with instruments of every kind, all moving together in perfect harmony.

Indeed, I was playing the cello. Playing it, being played by it, or just being it—I'm not sure which. One minute the instrument was beneath my fingers, the next, I pulled a bow over the hairs on my belly. Either way, a cello's rich tones poured out of me, as my own voice, merging gloriously with the music around us.

As the sun set, its last golden rays shot through a sky filling with rich pinks and purples, deep oranges and yellows. The beauty of the scene crescendoed with the music as small, black notes—quarter notes, half notes, sixteenth notes—began to appear above every instrument and each voice.

Notes poured out of my own cello like a scene from an animated movie. They gathered in the sky above us, all of the notes flocking together like birds. Then they became actual birds, a flock with sudden shifts, then shifts within shifts, as though dancing to our music. The colors of the setting sun intensified behind them.

Carried by bliss, I left myself standing on the hillside with the cello and became a note, swirling ecstatically through the sky. The other notes around me flashed with different colors and patterns, then blended together. I moved with them, as them. Upward I rose, joining so completely with everyone and everything around me that I lost myself in this homage and became One with Source. In rapture, I disappeared.

10

The Seven Senses

"These understandings can trigger a leap in
development for one who is ready to leave
the safety of the known haven for
the mysteries of Heaven."

~ Aion

When I came back to myself, I was standing on an asteroid in the
dark of space. The horizon was very close, the terrain around
me rocky and without grass or other familiar signs of life.

Just an instant before, I had completely merged with Source in the
most profound experience of music I had ever known. Coming out of
it like this—alone on an empty rock floating through space—hit me
hard. What was going on? Had I been kicked out of Heaven?

"Stevie, let go and go deeper," the silky female voice said, answering the questions I hadn't spoken. "You are only perceiving these
things with your seven senses."

Then it hit me. Seven senses? I held my hand to my face. It appeared so clearly that I could see the lines on my palm and the whorls
of each fingerprint. I counted on each finger: taste, touch, smell,
sight, hearing.

"But I only count five senses," I returned. "What are you talking
about?"

"Your sixth sense," she explained, "is your sense of knowing. We
wish you would trust that more."

"Your seventh sense is your sense of empathy," she went on to say.
"It's what we've been working on with you here."

It was incredible. I had rarely thought about this experience since it happened. But more than 30 years later, I was now receiving the same guidance from Aion.

The sixth sense is soul knowing.

Trust that your sixth sense guides your choices. It encompasses insight, intuition, embedded knowledge, foresight, psychic aware-ness, hunches, and precognition. Insights are realizations before thought. Feelings, emotions, sensations, images, and unspoken words are used by Spirit to provide guidance, warnings, and hints for a more joyful and spiritually connected life. Your ability to speak clearly with us arises from this innate sixth sense.

You've been learning to trust your soul connection over the past few decades. Understand that your trust allows us to transmit the thought packets to you and unlock your innate soul knowing, enabling your translation of our messages.

From your side, it seems that the knowing was already there, and it was. But you didn't realize it until you made the translation. There is no need to worry if you're getting it right, only to surrender your ego-mind to the process.

The seventh sense is resonance. Resonance keeps you empa-thetically connected to those physically around you as well as all souls you cannot see who are vibrating on similar frequencies.

We employ nature, music, people, animals, and all kinds of angelic help to provide you with signs and miracles that fuel your intuition and resonance.

Do miracles really happen?

Miracles do happen, though they most often go unrecognized. Miracles are a matter of viewpoint. From the sea level of human consciousness, miracles seem to revolve around the individual. But from our altitude, miracles move the masses to higher planes of consciousness in unimaginable and magnificent ways. One per-son's heart generates ripples through creation in ever-expanding circles of joy. Now that's a miracle!

I thought of what had happened next on my journey so long ago. It had been the kind of miracle Aion described.

"Who are you?" I had asked my guide, still standing on a lonely asteroid. "What is your name?"

"Ha-ha-ha-ha-haaa!" she responded, her laugh like a brook flowing over stones.

I looked up and saw that a star in the sky above me was moving. I realized it was coming toward me. But instead of getting bigger, the bright white light was shrinking, condensing. As it drew closer and closer, it continued to coalesce.

"Stevie," my guide explained, her voice a little further away now, "this is a gift to you from the Father."

Suddenly the light was right in front of me. It was smaller than a golf ball, a self-effulgent sphere of luminous energy. Reaching out, I cupped my hands.

"This is the pearl of great price," she continued, her voice becoming even more distant. "Keep it with you always."

I held it in my hands. Energy streamed into my wrists, my arms, my whole body. Drawing my hands to my heart, I watched the ball of light disappear into my chest.

"Keep it with you always." She was fading out. "Keep it with you always.... "

"Wait, wait! I don't where I am. I don't know how to get back."

"What do you mean? You have the pearl of great price," she responded from somewhere far away.

"Where are you going?" I was getting scared. "Don't leave me."

She laughed. "Leave you? But where could I go? You have the pearl of great price."

"What is your name?" I insisted. "Please tell me your name so I can call you."

One last time, she laughed delightedly, then faded away.

As my guide's voice faded, the space around me went black. Suddenly I found myself falling down the shaft again. Then—zoop!—I popped out. I was standing in front of Arlington House Hospital, a private psychiatric facility where I had worked as a counselor in my twenties. I walked through the glass front door without opening it, like a ghost.

Stepping into the day room, I noticed a very thin, uptight woman. Her fear was so strong that I could see it radiating out of her forehead in concentric black circles. She looked at me, and our eyes locked. No one else could see me but her.

"Oh, my God!" she exclaimed, her eyes wide and fixed on me.

"Hey," I responded, keeping my tone light. "You can see me."

"Who are you?" she asked nervously. "Where did you come from? Can you help me?"

Somehow her whole story came into me and I understood. She had experienced a psychic opening and could see into other dimensions. But she couldn't tell the difference between these other dimensions and the waking world. I could see that she was actually not going crazy, even though she was convinced of it. Fear paralyzed her.

"Let go," I said, "and go deeper. You are only experiencing these things with your seven senses."

She nodded, as if she understood.

With this, the scene disappeared. I was surrounded by blackness, then back in my body, which was still asleep. I urged my body to awaken and slowly arose, refreshed and revitalized from my journey.

At the time, this experience impacted me deeply. It would be years before I understood that my guide's name was Laughter, a presence so close that I truly could call on her any time, simply by having a good laugh. But even before this awareness came, I had learned through my journey that I could find the guidance I needed within myself. It gave me the courage to step into the unknown.

My first journey through the landscape of the seven senses had ultimately culminated in service, the same place that Aion's instruction would guide me to these many years later.

Stevie, your task is to use your seven senses to align your many selves and unify your field. Your talent is to help others do the same. By gathering them into groups, you have the ability to bring large numbers of people onto the path. We need all the help we can get to bring Earth's transition to a triumphant conclusion, elevating the earth plane to its next level of consciousness.

What does the transition look like? What will it look like when it is complete?

It will never be complete until all souls have rejoined Source. However, this stage of evolution in consciousness is accelerating and unfolding beautifully and perfectly. The transition is, of course, an elevation in frequency for all souls on Earth, for the Earth itself, and for all beings throughout the multiverse.

This movement into an increased vibration begins with the souls on Earth and will ripple out from there into all dimensions. During the transition, all souls will have an opportunity to find a new place for themselves in the multiverse, a new path of development, and a new, more etheric vibration of love. All will grow in consciousness as is appropriate for their state of development. Many changes on many levels will occur. Some already have.

Are these the end times you are talking about?

Yes, indeed it will seem like an end to some, but for most it will be a new beginning. It is a shift, a change in the perception of what reality is. From one perspective, an old view of reality will be ending. Common social beliefs, governmental institutions, religious dogma, scientific measures of reality, and some so-called physical laws will all be called into question by the direct experience of a higher spiritual vibration.

For those unwilling to let go of these cornerstones of current civilization, these events will be very unsettling. Resistance to the direct experience of Spirit as well as clinging to strongly held but outmoded beliefs will congest their energy systems and cause some discomfort until they can dissolve and discharge the blockages.

Why do humans have such a hard time letting go? Why does walking the path of transformation seem so scary?

Souls are most comfortable with what they believe they know. This is fine, and we have compassion for all souls, for all are on the journey back to Source. But residing only in what you believe or think you know restricts the joy of self-realization.

All souls are on the same path and seek to merge with the eternal Source from which they sprang. They are just temporarily at different rest stops along the way. Temporarily means a brief time, which is no time at all.

Aion, do you really mean everyone? From my perspective, it seems like some people really are stuck and not interested in evolving.

The words, images, and understandings here are appropriate for every being at some time in their journey toward the true experience of their own divine nature. But that time is not linear. These understandings can trigger a leap in development for one who is ready to leave the safety of the known haven for the mysteries of Heaven.

Rest assured, the path is safe even if it is not always comfortable, and we are here to guide and encourage every being to take the next step. We laud the courage of those who consciously choose to walk the path of transformation.

From the perspective of those who are already integrating Spirit energy into their everyday consciousness, these times will be a glorious ride. Finally, earth souls will be easily able to bridge both worlds. Daily life will be a true expression of Spirit's love, compassion, healing, and growth. Expressing divinity will be the way of life on the planet.

Earth will behave as planets do, shifting in many aspects to reflect its celestial place in this universe. Shifts in rotation and electromagnetic energy, shifts in its fiery core, its earthen crusts, salty seas, and swirling air will change the climate and, thus, the face of the planet. This is natural and has been going on for ages. It is not a problem. People will have to adjust, and it may be uncomfortable for some. They might choose to leave and find a more suitable place for their evolution.

Earth is in a continual state of evolution on a time scale that humans have only just begun to understand. It has been too slow for people to notice. The minute adjustments and interactions of all the forces acting on the planet tend to go unrecognized until they precipitate in eruptions, tsunamis, undersea tectonic shifts, earthquakes, electromagnetic storms, magnetic shifts, typhoons, tornados, and other manifestations of Earth's power to evolve that are just too big to ignore.

It is the evolution of human consciousness that is the most important shift. The love light emanating from so many now is changing the frequency of the overall human vibration. Their soul integration is changing the nature of life on Earth. By bringing the vibration of Spirit to Earth and elevating human consciousness into Spirit, they are shifting the energy of this entire plane. This is creating a new reality that brings a time of Heaven on Earth, a new beginning. Life is not ended; it is merely changed.

I suggest you and all other humans become experts at change. This transition has already begun. All souls are already choosing how to respond, even if unconsciously. Be conscious of your choices.

Be a bridge between both worlds, become a master of energy transformation, and enjoy the ride!

II

Speaking Up

"It's not the words but the vibration, the resonance
of Spirit that is important and does
the work of transformation."

~ Aion

The instructions from Aion on my talent and my task felt huge. On one hand, I knew to the core of my being that indeed it was my life's work to gather others together to support the shift happening on the planet. Toward this end, I wanted to offer other people a chance to receive personal messages from Aion just as I had. But it seemed like a huge stretch beyond my current ability. How would I even begin?

Aion, I know you told me my work is to bring people together for transformation, and your wisdom has been so transformative for me. I would like to give others the opportunity to ask you personal questions, just as I have, letting them speak to you through me. But I also find the idea of speaking your transmissions out loud somewhat daunting.

The truth is, you can share our messages out loud already. We can hear you! You are coming through loud and clear on our side, and we are coming through clearly on yours.

Giving voice on your plane to these conversations is a simple and easy next step. You may be nervous at first, but trust us. We guarantee success in your initial public transmission. You do the breathing and we'll do the speaking. You can even correct us if you like. We are often verbose, while you are more succinct. You make us look good!

Thanks, Aion. But I still feel like I have a lot to learn. What can I do to prepare myself for a project like this?

You can get over yourself. By this we mean, let go of the fear of doing a poor job in front of other people. It's true that you have learned to improve your word choices by practicing through writing. Now try speaking aloud. Your word choices will be a bit less considered and reconsidered, but the power and meaning of the message will still come through.

It's not the words but the vibration, the resonance of Spirit that is important and does the work of transformation. After all, it is the effect, not the rhetoric, that we are after. On Earth, people put too much emphasis on the words over the meaning and experience. Religions fall into this trap, creating much strife and wasted lifetimes. But I digress.

Learning to Speak Guidance Aloud

As you practice, try thinking in whole sentences before you speak, rather than just individual words and phrases. To begin, ask us for images that form a complete thought, one idea at a time. These you can translate into sentences. As you improve, you can receive larger image clusters that you can convert into entire paragraphs.

Let's practice now. Take three deep breaths and exhale slowly after each one. Your eyes can be open or closed. We will begin giving you whole, single thoughts. As you receive them, inhale, forming a sentence in your mind. At the top of the breath, we will help by confirming or correcting the sentence you formed. On the exhale, speak the sentence, then type it.

Ready? OK, here we go. Don't worry. There's nobody here but us chickens.

Just as Aion instructed, I took three deep breaths. With this, I received the first sentence of the message, which I spoke out loud, then typed.

"We are gathered here, in love, to help you bring forth teachings to transform the earth plane to its next level."

Wow, I thought. *This is really working.* On the next inhale, I received another sentence. On the out breath, I said:

"Levels are vibration frequencies that correspond to levels of consciousness."

During the next sentence, I noticed that Aion was fleshing out the idea while I was speaking about it. I spoke the opening phrase:

"The universe.... "

While I spoke, Aion sent another image to clarify my understanding. I saw not one universe, but many, intersecting like layers of soap bubbles in a tub. I added a new phrase to reflect this clarification from Aion.

" ....the entire multiverse is participating in this effort."

Cool. I was learning to translate Aion's messages into the spoken word. The image clusters were coming much faster now, with shorter pauses between them. I finished my first verbal transmission.

"We celebrate your efforts and the efforts of all humanity, and we await your arrival in full consciousness with great expectations and excitement."

Phew, what a relief! I had done it. I had spoken Aion's guidance aloud, in the moment. Before it happened, I could not even imagine how to do it. Now I was soaring. My heart swelled with gratitude, both for the beauty of the message and the support for being able to speak it.

There, you see; this isn't so bad. Nor is it difficult. It's OK to go slowly at first and build speed later. Our job is to send you clear transmissions through the veil.

When you get stuck or lose your focus, simply take three deep breaths, pause, and begin again. Simple, isn't it?

Yes, it is simple, but complex, too. Is this how everyone doing this kind of work receives messages from Spirit?

Not exactly. Everyone has their own process, but they are all receiving thought packets, the clusters of information we send you. People who receive these packets translate them into pictures, words, and feelings, or into a combination of them, in their own way.

In general, this approach to translating our messages is a good way to begin. You don't have to worry about delivering the teachings perfectly. Even as we help you speak our messages, we are helping listeners receive and understand their meaning. No need to feel overly responsible for their experience.

Am I bringing through messages just from you, or also my guides and angels, or even my Higher Self?

We'll, it doesn't make a difference. In fact, this is an example of getting hung up on words rather than meaning or experience. Your distinctions are meaningless; that is, on our side, the distinctions are meaningless. Your voice is our voice. We are one. We act as a collective consciousness.

It's another one of our paradoxes. We are simultaneously one and separate entities. We have personalities, but no Source energy gets lost in the translation from the One to the individual being. Your requests are received by one and all, and the All in One.

Spirit hears and answers your every prayer, and Spirit is everywhere. But your frequency determines whom you hear. The higher your frequency, the higher the frequency of the message you receive, the closer that message will be to Source. Each soul receives according to its abilities.

Can I teach this?

Yes. Remember, you aren't doing the teaching alone. We are all on the same team.

Even with Aion's encouragement, I still felt intimidated by the prospect of sharing what until now had been private, written conversations out loud in front of a group. But I knew that I would have to come out of the closet sooner or later and translate Aion's messages for other people, regardless of how I felt about it.

Less than two weeks later, I did just that. For a small group of friends, I offered a transmission from Aion. This experience was both powerful and challenging.

I began with a verbal transmission to the group, made up of spiritual students, healers, and psychics. This part of the program was both effortless and elegant. After a clear discourse, Aion led the group in an exercise targeting their needs as healers. He directed them to raise and expand their frequencies, then to embrace and love themselves, just as they were so often doing for their clients.

But what happened next took me by surprise. I heard Aion, using my voice, say to the group, "Despite Stevie's nervousness, we will answer questions now."

With this, I heard my own inner voice. "Noooooo!" it was wailing. "Not that!" But I was on the spot. I took three deep breaths, then Aion asked for questions.

Fortunately, this process went smoothly—that is, until the very last person in the group asked her question. The transmission that came through for her was very clear. But I watched her struggle with the answer. She asked another question, and Aion gave another answer. But she didn't seem to be accepting the guidance coming through for her.

Now I was becoming concerned. I wanted her to have a good experience. I could feel my own energy getting tangled up with hers.

Just then, I got a very clear download. In 3-inch-high block letters scrolling across my field of vision, came these words: "END OF TRANSMISSION." I relayed this message to the group, and the energy in my field dissapated. The session was clearly over.

The woman I had been speaking to said, "End of transmission? Whoa, we got zapped!" Together we all laughed.

I left the experience with mixed feelings. On one hand, I knew that I had turned a corner in my relationship to Aion and this practice. What a delight it was for me to see people I cared about receiving so much from their interaction with Aion.

Still, I regretted the way the last part of this transmission had played out. While it was happening, I had gotten nervous about the way my friend was receiving the message. A part of me really wanted her to get it, to understand and accept Aion's guidance. I had been so concerned about it, in fact, that I lost my focus on Aion's frequency. Afterwards, I felt chagrin at letting myself get pulled out of the process so easily.

The next day, I sat down with my laptop to talk with Aion about it.

Hi again, Aion. Thank you so much for my first group conversation with you. Your love and compassion were evident, and your words had a powerful impact on the group. They loved your sense of humor.

Well, it was you doing the work. We were doing what we always do. Thank you for putting yourself out there. You did a fine job.

I know I began to think at times, which seemed to get in the way. It was almost like it weakened the signal until I lost the call.

Yes, your concern for how people were taking the answers to their personal questions led to a "dropped call," abruptly terminating the transmission. But overall, this is an excellent start in publicly sharing our message.

Rather than concerning yourself with the reactions of others, focus on translating the thought packets as thoroughly as possible.

Remember that everyone is responsible for what they experience, what they see, hear, feel, and understand, including the beliefs they hold, energy they can contain, and actions they take. Regardless of how masterful a job you do, their choices determine what they receive from the session.

Finally, relax! This is not a Broadway show. These sessions are you being your Higher Self, in the moment, in all your vulnerability and all your power. Remember, you are backed up by the best team in the multiverse! The session in front of others will go more smoothly when you relax and allow us to do the driving.

This comes with practice. Ask us to help you in any instance. Stay focused and open to our guidance, and it will go perfectly every time. You have nothing to defend or promote. Those who resonate to the teachings and the energy of the transmissions will be drawn to you. Others will not.

The space between words is as full of meaning as the words themselves. Presence blossoms in that space. Consciousness expands to fill it, bringing in energy from the connectedness it generates. Spirit energy attenuates time and opens the soul to its timeless nature. These realizations and the energy behind them are the core experiences for transformation.

It is the energy that transforms most of all. Those who live in that energy will be healed. Let everyone know we are available to them at all times for their support and advancement.

12

Healing with the Unified Field Meditation

"A unified field is like a large dish antenna for receiving and radiating healing energy in waves that ripple throughout the cosmos."

~ Aion

The instructions from Aion on my talent and my task felt huge. In one way, I knew to the core of my being it was my life's work to heal myself and help others do the same. But I still had so many questions.

One answer I received was a practice called The Unified Field Meditation. Just as a rushing river starts as a small stream, my first small experience grew into an essential daily practice at the heart of my own healing.

What is the best way for me to work with people to help them heal?

First, realize it is not you doing the healing. Healers are conduits for Spirit, bridging the flow of energy between worlds. In whatever form the healing comes, and it always comes, it is a gift from Spirit in partnership with the soul experiencing the healing.

The human soul teams up with other powerful beings. The soul's aspects, spirit guides, and angels make up the team to deliver the perfect healing for that soul. Together they provide the necessary factors for that soul to get closer to realizing its purpose.

They do so only because the soul in need of healing asked for help. Remember, help people heal only when they ask for it.

Consult with us anytime if you have questions about how to approach a healing. We are always here to help you determine the best way to proceed. Entering into another's healing process can be tricky because so much of healing is unseen and may rely on a string of choices made by the person over time. The healer is a part of this team but cannot control what the healing will actually be or when it might occur.

A healer is a pipeline for special frequencies of energy that are a perfect match with the soul's request for assistance. Once you and the client are synchronized, Spirit will help you both raise your frequencies to create a healing. This energy transfusion catalyzes a chain of healing opportunities. It sets the soul on a new path of possibilities for change, growth, and all kinds of healing in the physical, mental, emotional, subtle, and causal bodies.

All healings lead toward full integration with Source. Some healings are instantaneous, and some can take lifetimes. All paths to healing are open to every soul in every moment.

You know what to do already. Just release your fear and trust in your Higher Self. Healings will follow. You have the knowledge, skill, and experience to get started. Just don't over-promise. As we discussed, the soul group is doing the healing, and you are simply one member of the team.

You will use sound, singing, storytelling, hypnosis, hands-on energy work, and therapeutic techniques to help people release blocks and clear their fields. Simply bring them into the present moment, and we will help you help them. You may want to transmit Spirit guidance for them if they ask for it. This information will serve you, too. When you heal others, you heal yourself. We in Spirit are healed as well.

As the client's skill in clearing increases, she will learn to hold the new frequency and will not need your help to jumpstart her energy shift. Then she can proceed on her own.

Increasing the amplitude of energy and raising the frequency of your clients are the twin goals of healing. Your own ability to modulate your frequency to match the client's will accelerate the healing process. To achieve this, you will have to stay clear yourself. This doesn't mean you have to be perfect, but you must be present to do any good for another. Take care of yourself, body, mind, and spirit. Contact us everyday since that allows us to aid you in clearing.

We here in Spirit are a vast resource for you to utilize. Don't be shy. We know you're not! Ask us to help you clear, and you'll be surprised at how much better you will feel, how much clean, clear, healing energy will be flowing through you. It's better than an energy drink. Coffee just can't compare.

How can I best heal myself?

You understand spiritual energy, but you don't pay as much attention to it as you might. Somehow, spiritual energy takes a backseat to physical, emotional, and mental preoccupations. This is natural, but it is less than helpful for elevating your frequency and healing yourself. In fact, it is just the opposite of what you need to do to lead a lifetime of joy and connectedness. If your heart isn't bursting with love and gratitude, there is still room for improvement.

If you want to heal, increase your spiritual energy by simply putting your attention on it. Give it the kind of time, attention, and focus you give to earning a living or even, say, reading or watching television. This will transform your life in ways you can't even imagine.

The human energy system is a perfect instrument for translating spiritual energy into its corresponding expression on Earth. This includes drawing healing energy into your physical and subtle bodies. Your seven major chakras are an important aspect of these subtle or energy bodies because they serve as instruments for receiving, metabolizing, and transmitting energy. When all aspects of your many bodies vibrate in resonance, they create an interpenetrating, unified energy field. This is the field of light that surrounds all souls. This field is as much a part of you as your physical body.

A unified field is like a large dish antenna for receiving and radiating healing energy in waves that ripple throughout the cosmos. Vibrating as a unified field, you can live in complete resonance with

rit as a bridge between Heaven and Earth. A unified field is fun-
mental for evolving in consciousness, the most important state
to master in your life on Earth. The more attention you devote to
unifying your field, the more you will expand and raise its vibration,
creating a chakra amplification process with momentum of its own.

There are many ways to do this. Allow us to guide you through
a practice for unifying your field so you can be a clear conduit of
healing energy for Spirit on Earth.

The Unified Field Meditation

First, be sure you are in a quiet and comfortable place where
you will not be disturbed. You can be sitting or lying down, but stay
awake.

The meditation has three parts. The first is clearing the chakras
downward, from the crown to the ground. The second is filling up
with light to energize and unify the chakras into one field. The third
is to expand your unified field outward in all directions to resonate
with Spirit.

To prepare, open to Spirit energy by remembering or imagining
a magnificent, joyous moment. Let the energy of this moment fill
you from head to toe. Use this memory to expand the love in your
heart, to increase the energy in your field, and to open even more
to the light of your Higher Self.

Now ask us to guide you to raise your frequency and unify your
field. Set this intention clearly. We are always here to help and will
honor your intention. Know you can always attain the level of energy you seek, and you remain safe under our guidance.

Begin the first part of the meditation by clearing the chakras
from the crown, down through the balls of the feet and into the
ground.

Imagine or sense a ball of golden white light above you, shining down like the sun on the crown of your head, where your field
meets the One Field. Feel the light warming, relaxing, and illuminating the space at your crown. Sense into it. Accept whatever you
notice there, just as it is. Then set the energy of your crown chakra
spinning to the right, opening to the higher amplitudes of light

shining down from above. As you spin the energy, simply allow the opening to happen, letting light pour down into your energy body, clearing the crown chakra.

As I followed Aion's instruction, I found myself looking down on my body from above it. The space over my head was a single vortex opening upward. It spun clockwise, pulling the light from above me down into my field.

Now allow the amplified energy to naturally overflow from the crown, cascading down to your forehead, front and back. Again, feel the golden white light warming, relaxing, and illuminating the space there. Sense into it, accepting whatever you find, just as it is. Then set that energy spinning clockwise. Spin away anything that blocks or congests your energy, releasing it back to Source in order to open to greater insights, clearing the third eye.

In this way, Aion guided me to clear each chakra in turn. At each one, I saw two energy centers, one on the front and the other on the back of my body. I spun these energy centers clockwise each time, as if I wore a large clock on my chest with its hands moving to my left first, then around. When one chakra cleared, which I could gauge by my own sense of relief, I felt the energy overflow into the next chakra below it.

The third eye energy overflows into the throat chakra, opening it to higher levels of expression.

This energy cascades into the magnificent heart chakra, opening it to more love.

That heart light overflows into the solar plexus, opening it to greater expressions of your will.

The solar plexus spills over into the sacral area below the navel, amplifying creativity, co-creativity, and sacred sexuality.

Then that wave of light flows down to the root chakra at the base of the spine, opening it to a greater embodiment of Spirit in the flesh.

Finally, allow that light to continue down through the hips, thighs, and calves to the balls of the feet, sending a beam of light all the way to the center of Mother Earth to ground your system. Connect light from above into Earth below through the vessel of you, as a bridge between worlds.

Feel the vibration of energy as it moves through you, energizing, healing, and elevating your frequency. As it increases, you may sense it as a vibration, an embracing warmth, an enveloping light, or a soothing hum. Allow yourself to feel both relaxed and energized, expanded in Spirit and also present in the body, in awe of Spirit's loving energy and at one with it.

As light poured from the crown of my head, down the ladder of my seven chakras and through my feet, I felt like I was standing on soft, green turf, caressed from above by a sunny spring shower. Energy flowed through me more freely than I had ever experienced.

Now begin the next phase of this practice, filling up with light to energize, expand, and unify the chakras.

Bring your attention to the balls of your feet. Allow golden white light to fill your body the way water fills a glass.

First fill the feet, calves, and thighs, up to your hips, with light. Now breathe light into your root chakra at the base of the spine, allowing it to fill and expand. This light charges your root chakra, boosting it into a higher frequency. Allow the root chakra to expand until it contacts the sacral chakra above it. See the root chakra overlap with and activate the sacral chakra.

Now bring your attention to the sacral chakra. Allow it to fill with golden white light. Energize and expand the sacral chakra with this light, blending it with the root chakra. With your love and attention, unify the root and sacral chakras.

Continue filling up the sacral chakra until it expands into and activates the solar plexus. Fill the solar plexus with light now, energizing and blending it with the root and sacral chakras.

Step by step, Aion continued to guide me through the process of filling, expanding, and unifying the chakras, moving upward this time, seeing each chakra overlap with the next as it expanded. As energy moved, I felt myself tingling and vibrating all over. Aion continued.

Bring light up from below, down from above, and into every cell, connecting the root with the crown. Unify your field, linking earth below with Spirit above through the vessel of you, as a bridge between worlds.

And now begin expanding your field outward to resonate with Spirit. Draw your attention to your central core, allowing even more golden white light to pour into your system. Allow this energy to fill and penetrate all your bodies, from the cells of your physical body, all the way out to the edges of your energy field. Feel the spherical-shaped energy body expanding outward from the spinal column, through the organs and bones, past the skin and beyond, stretching out into the space around you.

In this resonant state, you can ask for healing, guidance, or simply commune with us.

Waves of warmth and energy radiated from my core. I could sense this energized field all around me, penetrating my body and nourishing my soul.

Stay with this feeling, and breathe even more light gently into it. Allow Spirit to bathe you, caress you. We can see you, a beautiful, luminous, golden sphere radiating all the way to our side of the veil. Learn to hold this vibration and stay in this resonant state. In it, you can ask for guidance and healing and even travel consciously to our side.

For now, simply enjoy this love and peace. Focusing on love, joy, and gratitude makes this an ecstatic reunion, dissolving all fear. This shower of energy is a gift from us to help you increase your capacity for aliveness.

Unable to contain so much ecstasy, tears of joy rolled down my face. How could I even begin to receive all this love?

As you build capacity to hold more energy in your system, you'll be able to stand and walk in this state and still function in your dimension. Talking and walking with eyes open while maintaining this high, resonant frequency is a good indication you are ready for the next stage.

What stage is that?

Growing toward full embodiment of Spirit in the flesh. We are bathing you in a spiritual light wave, washing you clean of anything that holds you back from realizing a magnificent life as Spirit. You and all souls are capable of this. You are a celestial being, so embrace yourself as Spirit as well as human.

Hold this elevated frequency and these exalted feelings. Enhance and amplify them. Unifying your field for 15 minutes each day is enough to transform your entire experience of human life. Imagine what twice a day could do. Practice unifying your field until you can do it in a single breath, or simply by saying, "Field, unify!"

This is how all souls evolve back to Source. Call on us, your loving spirit guides, to help you. We are always at your side, dear one. And we have your back, too. We in Spirit invite you to experience the divine light flowing through you. It is limitless energy and consciousness. In this state, there are many doors open to you. Which door will you open?

The Unified Field Meditation is the core practice of the teachings of Aion. For a free audio version of this practice, along with more detailed instructions, visit:
www.StevieRayMcHugh.com

13

As Big As Galaxies

"Be big! Be as big as galaxies, as magnificent as the
Milky Way. You already contain them all
because you come from Source
and are One with Source."

~ Aion

Aion, *my contact with you is transforming me by elevating my energy, my vibration. I am experiencing a deeper peace. My food cravings are changing. Fruits and vegetables have much more appeal now. I'm not feeling any craving for alcohol, which is amazing all by itself. My anxiety level has decreased substantially, and I feel happier than I have in many years—and I mean belly-laughing-out-loud happy. Thank you for this shift.*

Oh, it's you who is doing the heavy lifting here. We guide and nudge, but you're the one taking each step forward into the unknown. That's the real deal.

Your choices will always carry you to the next thing. What you choose, what you do with your light-of-awareness, your consciousness, determines what that next thing is.

Can it really be so simple? My intention, my attention determines my life?

Yes. Changing your life is simple but not necessarily easy. In the river of consciousness, there are many eddies. A soul can choose to remain in any one of them for lifetimes if the swirling side-current seems interesting enough.

What's the secret?

Put your attention on Spirit in the Here and Now. Intend to learn and grow on Earth and to develop your soul in Spirit. Be in the world and in Spirit.

I'm not saying to be in the world but not of it. This creates a split that later must be healed in order to be in the moment. Simply be in this moment fully. Take advantage of this time in a body and embrace life in the present. Presence is all it takes to realize the true nature of the multiverse.

I'm feeling such ecstasy.

Yes, ecstasy.

I see now that ecstasy is the true nature of the universe.

That's what we're saying, and now you know. Of course, you knew this before but forgot. More accurately, you got distracted, interested in other attractions.

With the movement of divine energy through your system, your holes, your energy leaks are shrinking. Some have already been stitched closed. It is as though they were never there at all.

I have often felt like Swiss cheese, full of holes.

Those energy leaks make it difficult to amplify your power and raise your frequency. Ego-centeredness, desires, fear, insecurities, a weak sense of self-worth, wide swings of emotion, and many other manifestations of physical, emotional, and mental unbalance contribute to your energy permeability. This reduces the amplitude of the divine current flowing through your core. It clouds spiritual guidance and slows development. Energy congests instead of flowing nicely. Through leaks large and small, a human's energy capacity dribbles away.

I feel your healing energy within me now and through much of the day. What do I need to do to stay conscious of Spirit all the time?

Let's begin with attention. You can think of attention as the organ of consciousness. Unlike most other organs, it doesn't reside in a single place in the body. Instead, it is generated from the entire nervous system, including the brain and the endocrine system, neurotransmitters, and supporting organs such as the liver.

Attention is a whole-body function. As such, it requires special care and feeding. Lack of sleep, nutrients, or vitamins can rob even a healthy person of the ability to focus. Neurological, metabolic, and other disorders can weaken the ability to be attentive.

In addition to the physical aspects of attention, there is the will. You live in a free will zone. You can do whatever you will. Will is intent. It is the lens of attention, the focusing mechanism of consciousness. Where the will is placed, so goes the consciousness. These are inseparable. Mental, emotional, and spiritual disorders can weaken the will, crippling your will to focus.

To stay conscious of Spirit all the time is an act of attention, an act of will. "Pay attention to what?" you ask. Ah, but you already know what! Nonetheless, I will walk you through it.

Pay attention to your energy on all levels. Use your senses to stay aware of everything around and within you.

How are you feeling physically? Do you need to eat, rest, or exercise? Can you feel the warmth of the air around you? Hear the sounds of life's activities? Do you see the magnificent details of creation in the material objects nearby? Can you appreciate them?

Can you sense the fine hum of your Spirit body? Where do you feel it the strongest? Do you feel the tingles of Spirit's energy wafting down upon you, entering your every pore, your every cell? No? Then breathe, relax, quiet your thoughts, and sense it. Breathe energy in to support and reinforce your vibration.

Do you feel empathy for and resonance with those around you? In your heart, in your gut, can you appreciate their struggles? Can you feel what they feel and still stay centered in your own emotions? Can you allow them to be who they are without judging or pitying, without holding on to or rejecting them?

Are you willing to know what you know? Can you integrate the lessons of the near and far past? How far back can you remember? Do you accept what you see and what you imagine of the near and the far future, which is yours to create? Can you know God in this moment?

Are you feeling me yet?

Yes, I'm getting the picture. And I'm feeling you strongly. You have quite a bit of intensity around the subject of attention. You certainly have my attention!

Holding all these points of attention is consciousness. Yes, this is big stuff. This is the stuff of God consciousness, total awareness, knowing, and compassion. Paying attention in this way will keep you conscious of Spirit.

Believe me; it is not too big for you or for anyone. It is your birthright and your soul destiny.

I feel like I cycle in and out of consciousness, paying attention then losing it.

Much of that cycle is due to distraction. But being distracted is a choice. Your attention follows your interests. The question is, what will you pursue? What do you want in this moment?

Just then, I took a sip of coffee.

That sip of coffee is delicious. Taste it fully, appreciate it while maintaining awareness of your energy body. Notice the taste amplifies the energy in your chakras, increases the spin, and raises the frequency a bit.

In this instance, the sip of coffee led you within, but it was your will to connect the taste to your energy body that made it so. You could also connect it outside of you, say, to your wife sitting next to you. You smile at her, reflecting the glorious taste, in appreciation of who she is and your love for her. This activates your heart center and raises your frequency again.

Going within and without, going inside and going outside, both can lead to contact with Spirit. It is just a matter of will and attention. No small matter!

Maintaining this degree of consciousness seems like a tall order. Is it even possible to sustain it while in a body?

Certainly. Yes, even by you, my son. Do you think you can get special dispensation? There is no shirking the expansion of consciousness.

There is every reason to grow in conscious awareness. The very best is because it accelerates the return to Source, but also for the ease, joy, and pleasure it brings to life, regardless of circumstances. Each moment contains sublime bliss when you are in it.

What about feeling pain and suffering?

Pain is experienced when you hold on to ego identifications. These identifications separate you from the joy of living in Spirit, in the Now. Suffering is attachment and identification with that pain. So suffering only exists when you are not in the present.

I believe you're talking about emotional, mental, or spiritual pain. What about physical pain?

The body's nervous system is finely tuned to provide feedback on a wide variety of levels. This feedback is to guide you back to God. The "you" who perceives the feedback notices the pain, but you are only controlled by it when identified with the physical body.

Those living with acute pain are facing the challenge of elevating their consciousness frequency to a very high point from which they no longer identify with the body's pain signals. It is not for you to understand why. This is their path. Just send light, love, and elevating thoughts to these people to help them on their own personal journey back to God.

The "you" who perceives is the soul?

Yes, the soul, which is inseparable from conscious awareness. I know, the notion of maintaining full awareness seems too big for you at this point, but, really, it only appears that way because that is the way you perceive it. In reality—yes, your earthly reality—consciousness is unlimited. All limitations are your own.

But my limitations seem so real to me. Please don't think I'm whining. I understand most of my excuses, and when I'm at my best, I don't totally buy in to them. But in the day-to-day of life on Earth, things like clothing, food, shelter, work, and health seem like practical necessities.

My brother Jesus said to be like the birds that neither toil nor spin. What do you think He was driving at?

My image of this is just dropping every material preoccupation and wholeheartedly pursuing the connection to Spirit.

OK, what does this look like to you?

Oh boy, this is going to take a while. Can I get back to you on this?

As you will.

I spent the rest of my day pondering this question, which I knew I needed to see from a fresh perspective. When I sat down again in the evening to dialogue with Aion, I was ready to offer the insights that had come to me.

If I understand correctly, what Jesus meant was to live in the moment, radiating gratitude, appreciating our aliveness and connection to Spirit, along with the beauty and bounty of Earth.
How'd I do?

You do seem to be getting it. You avoided the old trap of making false distinctions between the spiritual and the mundane.
Living in Spirit energy, living in the Now precludes nothing material. Living a life in Spirit doesn't mean you have to become

a monk as you did when you were young. Eventually, you clearly recognized the pitfall of spiritual materialism. The wily ego finds another way to create attachment, even when you are following all the accepted instructions for a spiritual life.

Appearances can deceive others, but not the Higher Self. Only those who are pure of heart, purely in the moment, acting without attempting to influence the future or change the past, can pass through the all-seeing eye of the needle.

I can see now that I have been going about my life all wrong. I've put every-thing before presence, striving to achieve the material dream. But my striving has turned the dream into a nightmare, one from my childhood where I am pushing, leaning into the wind of a hurricane, struggling to get home lest I be swept away.

This is why the Bible speaks about the awe of being in the presence of God. Was Moses thinking about his 401K in front of the burning bush? Of course not! He was simply present, in awe.

Experiencing God is awesome!

You have experienced the Divine Light of God. In those moments, you were 100 percent present, but still conscious, still able to get up in the morning. Right action springs from trusting the present, being present. Presence is a present from God to you, so you can know God. Open the present in this moment, and know you are God.

Whoa, that feels like a big leap.

Be big! Be as big as galaxies, as magnificent as the Milky Way. You already contain them all because you come from Source and are One with Source. Don't be afraid of what you are. Embrace the great expanse of your soul and consciousness.

Leave your concept of limited self. Step out of that and into your presence, full-bodied and fully connected. Feel the fullness. Trust your Higher Self and take action in the moment. Just see how it goes for a day, a week, a lifetime, even. Get back to me on that!

Thank you so much, Aion. You are opening my eyes to a true life.

14

You Are God Enough

*"There was no tree, no snake, and no apple.
I should know; I was there."*

~ Aion

At age 20, I read *Be Here Now*, the famous book by Ram Dass. It catapulted me into a whole new way of seeing the world. I began doing yoga for two hours a day, and I found Parmahansa Yogananda's book *Autobiography of a Yogi*, a profound inspiration for me at the time. My life became a spiritual quest.

During that period, I had taken a job in construction as a day laborer—not the easiest gig for the skinny boy I was then. After one particularly hard day of work, hand-mixing cement and carrying concrete blocks, I rode my bike 10 miles home, ate my dinner of beans and rice, and collapsed into bed.

What happened next is difficult to put into words. I didn't even really lie down; I just leaned back against the pillows. Almost immediately, I was transported to another place, a state of mind something like a lucid dream, but even more vivid.

I found myself standing in the back of an auditorium, its sloping floor lined in rows of chairs leading to a proscenium stage with lighting and curtains. The house was packed. People around me chatted in their chairs, all of us waiting for someone to make an entrance.

Finally, a little bald-headed man in saffron robes and tiny black shoes came out. Scanning the crowd, he looked straight at me, locking his eyes on mine. Energy started coursing through my system. I was mesmerized.

In my waking life, I had been reading Meher Baba's book *True Discipleship*. In it, he states that when you kiss the feet of the guru, grace flows into your soul. But I didn't care what kissing someone's feet would do for me. When I read it, I swore I would never kiss anyone's feet, no matter who it was.

Now, here I was, in the presence of this tiny Indian man I'd never seen. Just like Yogananda, all I could think was, my guru is calling me! In that moment, all I wanted was to throw myself at his feet.

I started running toward the front, as the little Indian man walked to the edge of the stage. But about halfway down the aisle, a huge weight crashed down on my shoulders. I came skidding to a halt on my knees in one of those slow-motion moments that can only happen in dreams. Time moved like molasses around me. All I wanted was to bow and touch those shoes, my guru's feet.

From somewhere above me, a voice boomed. "You can't do this. If you do, you'll die. And besides, you're not worthy."

But I had to touch those feet. Now I was crawling on all fours, getting closer, energy pouring through me. I looked up at the stage, and the man's heart turned into a golden circle, with the face of a young boy at its center. This image, which would later take on great significance for me, was both cryptic and compelling.

By now, my fingers were just inches away from those feet. "Keep your spine straight!" I coached myself. "You can do this!" The only thing I could see was a field of brilliant white light with two little black cloth shoes sticking out of it. I was reaching, stretching my whole body, straining toward the shoes.

But the voice came again. "No, you can't do this. If you do, you'll die. And besides, you're not worthy!"

On and on this went, me reaching, the voice refusing me, with what felt like hours passing, until the pain was so excruciating it woke me.

When I stepped into the bathroom, a blistered face stared back at me from the mirror. Yellow-brown patches of bubbled skin covered my ears, my cheeks, my nose. This was no sunburn. It couldn't be. I had spent my day under tree cover. But these were serious burns, pain shooting through my whole body from my face.

"Oh, my God!" I bellowed.

Hearing me exclaim, one of my housemates woke up and came in to check on me.

"Whoa! What happened to you?" he asked.

"I don't know," I told him. "I had this dream, and I woke up like this." I told him about the man, the shoes, the blazing white light.

"It must be nerves," he responded.

Nerves? Right.

Not long after, I heard about a teacher for Guru Maharaj Ji who was coming to Boston. I went with my best friend, Mitchell, to see him. My face, now peeling, still felt on fire, even though two weeks had passed since my dream. And when I went to receive the teacher's initiation into divine light, my third eye opened, energy coursed through my body, and the light began burning my face again as it had in the dream. In the middle of the initiation, I actually threw my hands up and called out, "No! Stop!" I still had no idea what was happening to me.

After this initiation, referred to in this lineage as "receiving knowledge," I saw a poster of Guru Maharaj Ji as a young child in front of a microphone at his father's funeral. It was the same child's face that had appeared in my dream. For me, seeing his face before I had ever heard of or physically met Guru Maharaji Ji felt like a sign that I had found my teacher.

But these intense encounters with white light continued. At the heart of the experiences and my own ambivalence toward them lay the deeply rooted feeling of unworthiness I had contacted so clearly in my dream. Eventually I would come to understand that the booming voice above me in my dream was not God speaking but the internalized voice of my demanding, war-traumatized father. Unworthiness became a common thread in my love-fear relationship with high-voltage kundalini energy and the spiritual transformation it brought.

Last night I was thinking about our conversation, and I recognized my resistance to your call for me to be big. I feel some fear around that. Can you help me release my fear?

Limitation has been all you have known since you were born. For many reasons and without laying any blame, it has become a habit of thought with which you identify.

Who are you without those thoughts? Habits are most easily replaced with new habits, thoughts, and behaviors to practice. But first you must become aware of the underlying thoughts and beliefs generating a habit. Then you must decide and whole-heartedly intend to release the limiting beliefs. This creates an energetic opening in your field for a new belief to take root, one based on living in the Now and the experience of Spirit.

Don't feel so glum, my friend. You can be too hard on yourself at times like this. We are helping you raise your frequency. On the one hand, this makes changing easier, but on the other, it shakes you loose from your habitual moorings. It is normal to feel a bit adrift in a period like this.

We are your anchor. Know that you will pass through this transformation, and you will.

I feel so good, so relieved hearing you say that. I know I can put my trust in you.

Actually, you are putting your trust in your Higher Self. Don't abdicate your own spiritual power to us. Turning your life over to us is not being big. We are your big brothers and sisters. You are one of us in a body. We can help, but you do the work.

My trust in me could be stronger.

Let's start here. What could lead you to a stronger trust in you?

I have failed so many times in so many ways. I feel terrible about that.

And have you succeeded?

Yes, I have succeeded about as many times as I have failed, if not more. Somehow the failures add up to a larger feeling than the successes. I fear for my future even as I feel so supported in our connection.

These discussions are providing me with a stronger core sense of self, an anchor in Spirit, but it is not strong enough yet to overcome my fear, my "not good enough" self-judgment and habitual worries.

You are God enough.

That's very kind of you to say, but...

Is this the resistance you were talking about earlier?

Oops. Yes, it is. So weak self-esteem is my underlying habitual belief?

Thoughts that you are not God enough, not good enough or worthy of love from Spirit, hold you back from the moment. It is the shame induced by the myth of original sin.

There was no tree, no snake, and no apple. I should know; I was there. The advent of human consciousness on Earth, the ego, and the veil created a false feeling of separation between the angelic world and human beings.

But there was and is no loss of love. It was not a fall from grace but a grand experiment by Source to know its Self. Humans are angels in the flesh. All who incarnated then, as now, chose to leave Spirit for a chance to evolve in a human form. In the shock of the transition, they blamed themselves for being kicked out of Heaven, but it is not the case, as you know deep in your heart.

You are free to choose your internal state of being. Make a habit of choosing high spiritual thoughts over and over again throughout your day and night. Look around you. What reminds you of God and your spiritual nature?

Contact our energy by breathing consciously, filling your energy body with light, then unifying and expanding your field. Lift up your thoughts. There is always a higher frequency to touch. This new habit will lead you to a stronger you, a more connected self.

I'm also concerned about my accuracy in translating your transmissions. The felt images are so powerful and inspiring, so beautiful and so healing. I know I don't always make the best word choices in the moment. I find myself going back to parts I struggled with and revising them to improve the translation.

Is that OK with you? How can I make better choices the first time? And how will I ever be able to transmit these healing energies from you to other people if I make mediocre choices?

Being perfect is not an option on this earth plane, so just let that go. Good enough in the moment is fine.

Words are slippery, which makes for great poetry but poor gospels. Your job is to get the concepts across and, when possible, to convey the energy experience of the concepts from us to the readers. It is up to us to send the thought packets to you in a form you can easily translate, given your current level of awareness. We are all working this out together.

Remember, this is the living Word. Just because the Ten Commandments and the Code of Hammurabi were carved in stone, people think each scribed word is sacrosanct. (That last one is a good word choice, by the way.)

Words have meaning, but often more than a single definition. And the meanings of words change considerably over time. These multiple meanings and usages add richness to language, making it better able to represent a wide range of perceptions. Language can blur or obscure some principles and realizations, but they are never completely lost in translation.

Misunderstanding is a risk we must take. We use repetition and energy transmission to transform bare bones concepts into vital, living realizations.

Stop doubting yourself and start speaking your truth. Continue breathing yourself into the sacred Now. This is not a time to be timid or falsely modest. This is a period of joyous exploration and realization.

To serve as a bridge between Spirit and Earth and assist others in discovering and expressing their true nature, you have to have the courage to allow your own transformation to unfold. Be with us in the bliss of this perpetual moment, and do that which sings for you. All else will follow.

All this feeds back into our earlier discussion on being God enough. Trust your connection, and your spiritual work will flow effortlessly, like water down a mountainside.

Thank you, Aion. This is most helpful. I feel better already.

Good. Stay in this blissful state as long as you can. You can return here at will.

Rest in peace. This advice is best practiced by the living!

15

Emotional Clearing

"Coat your irritations with a celestial frequency to grow your own pearl of great price."

~ Aion

When I closed my software company, I was disappointed and upset with myself, even dejected. But I was also secretly relieved. If my company had sold, I would have stepped into another high-pressure job that would require international travel, working with the product I had created. With the company and my product gone, I would not have to put myself under the same pressure that consulting had always meant to me: board rooms, hotel bars, boring dinners with people I didn't really like. The truth was, some part of me finally felt free.

Now, with this energy flowing through me from Aion, I was experiencing bliss as my day-to-day state of being. I knew I could not go back to that hard-driving corporate world, at least not yet. Not while this energy was so new for me. This state felt like a fragile sprout I needed to protect from the elements if it would survive.

This was a major shift. No longer was I identifying myself with my house or the brand-new Lexus hybrid in our driveway. For the first time in decades, my life was not about my career or what I could accomplish. Instead, I was spending all my time working with energy and light. Power and life moved through me in a way it never had.

But the impact of my choices was not always comfortable. Because I wasn't working, I wasn't making money. I was paying our mortgage out of my retirement savings, and my wife knew what this meant. We were on a track to financial disaster.

Understandably, this situation was not something she could easily accept. When we married, I had agreed to take care of her financially, and before the leg injury and collapse of my business, I had provided for us both in style.

With our financial situation deteriorating, the mounting tension between us was moving from a simmer to a boil. Even though we still rarely argued, our life began to feel like a pressure cooker. As I watched our frustrations build, I felt the energy leak out of our relationship, even as I still felt my love for her. I was nervous and worried about what would happen with us, but I had no idea how to handle it.

Hi, Aion. I'm sorry to say I'm feeling sad.

Indeed you are, my friend. No need to apologize. There is nothing wrong with feeling your feelings. In fact, it is the first step toward releasing them back to Source.

My sadness feels like stuck energy, a lump in the center of my chest.

Emotional Clearing Practice

Breathe into the lump. Feel whatever feelings are there. No need to name them, simply feel. With each successive breath, breathe into that area a little more deeply. Build a little more energy in and around the spot where the heavy, stuck feeling resides. After a few breaths, on the exhale, make a sound that sends a vibration into that area.

Keep breathing deeply into the area, then humming, toning, or making sounds that vibrate it. Allow the sound to change as the feeling changes. If the feeling shifts to a new spot, follow it with the breath and the sounds.

When the energy has begun to expand, bathe any area that is still tender in warm, golden light. Shine that healing golden light into it, and cradle it in a field of sound. You may begin to feel some compassion for this part of you. Give it a little more love, more attention. Breathe into it with tenderness.

Expand the energy like a balloon that gets thinner and lighter as it grows. As it thins, you may feel it changing into a charge of tingling energy. Take this charge and spread it throughout your whole energy field, dissipating the charge. Allow the energy to evaporate like dew in morning sun.

If anything remains of this old feeling and you are ready to release it, ask us to help you. Ask now. Feel a warm, tingly shower of golden light sprinkling down upon you, contacting the outer layers of your energy field to coat and illuminate it.

As this golden energy shower continues, feel the energy move deeper, saturating the field around your body, then entering the pores of your skin. Allow the golden light to fill your body, radiating through your organs, your bones, into the cells of your body.

Watch this grace-filled light as it cleanses the old, contracted energy from the cellular memory of your whole body. Soften the edges of your energy field, releasing any remaining discomfort like wisps of smoke flowing out of you, back to Source.

Gently relax now. Feel our presence, our love. Bring energy up from your feet, through the chakras to your forehead, and out the top of the crown. Connect your energy with a glowing, golden ball of light above your head.

Feel the stream of healing golden energy filling you now, down through the crown, down into your energy body, flowing down chakra by chakra to your feet, then into the ground.

Now cycle this stream of energy up from the ground again. Bring it up through the chakras, breathing into each chakra and connecting that chakra with the ball of golden light just above your head. You can continue cycling energy up from the ground, through each chakra, and to the crown, slowly building speed and raising your frequency on each pass.

Filled with golden white light from the inside, let yourself vibrate and resonate with us. Stay present with any sensations. Let the energy nourish and heal you.

Give thanks to God. You are healed.

I feel so good, so healed right now. My inclination is to get up and take some action, to do something to resolve my issue.

You have already resolved it. In fact, you dissolved it. You liquidated it, just as Dorothy dissolved the witch with a bucket of water. Simply enjoy how good you feel in this moment. Remember this state. You can return here at will. Just follow the yellow brick road!

You mean I don't have to do anything about this situation?

You mean about that situation you had?

You're right. It's gone. Or it may still be a situation, but I'm not feeling triggered by it. It is just not an issue for me. It's become something else, like someone else's dilemma that I don't have to solve because it will resolve on its own. I'm feeling very present and amazingly full, yet totally detached from that old issue.

The present moment will do that for you.

And your amazing, healing energy.

We are Aion and the Soul Guardians at your service.

Sounds like a rock band, doesn't it?

We rock.

You certainly rock me. Will this release process work all the time for me?

Most of the time, in most situations, yes. It will work for you as long as you work it. Again, you are healing yourself with an extra boost of energy from us. It is your intent to release, your willingness to move your energy that's the magic mojo. Without that, we can't do much for you. You know, you can lead a horse to water....

Are you saying it's not necessary to talk about or vent a pent-up emotion, to analyze its roots in family history, or to act it out in order to release it?

Not if you can move your energy by increasing its amplitude and raising your vibration. Especially not if you raise your vibration and ask for our help.

To get back to the previous question, the only times this won't work for you is when you can't, or think you can't, consciously access your energy. Physical, mental, or emotional shock or extreme energy depletion can make it more difficult, but not impossible.

Practice daily in all kinds of situations. Make expanding your energy and raising your frequency an automatic response, like hitting the brakes or the gas pedal while driving a car. Make it as natural as breathing. When you make it a spiritual habit, the ability will be there when you need it most.

Previously, we discussed energy modulation for living on both sides of the veil. That skill is an extension of dissolving stuck emotional energy.

So, Stevie, trust that it will all work out. Your worries and your fears hold you back. As we discussed, most worries and fears arise from a future orientation that keeps you on edge and out of the present. This constricts your energy and lowers your frequency. Below a certain threshold, this results in pain.

Do you see how easy it is to move out of fear? It's fast, too. Remember, the intent to clear and unify your field is the engine that powers the process. Now that your frequency is higher, we can get through to you more clearly.

Take some time each day to open to the magnificence of the Spirit world. It's a lot like lying down in the soft grass outside on a clear night and gazing up at the stars. Project yourself into our realm, and ask to be shown what you need to know in order to be of service to Spirit. You can simply say, "Please guide me for the highest good of my soul."

Where will I go?

You don't need to know your way around. You will be led by Spirit. Of course, you can call on us. We are always available for you.

You keep bringing up the notion of me visiting the other side as an important skill. Why?

Ah, my young padawan, you are still unaware of your abilities and important responsibilities. You will be happiest contributing at the high end of your ability as a bridge between worlds.

It seems so esoteric and, well, hard to do. I know I have passed into other dimensions several times over the last 40 years, but those experiences, while life-changing, have been very few and far between.

You can go there daily or nightly, for that matter. It's consciousness we want you to cultivate. For now, use the practices we have given you. But eventually you will be able to simply choose where you want to reside and be there. Doing this will give you the experience of things as they really are. All other life experiences pale in comparison to full consciousness.

Your life up until this point has been about collecting experiences. Now it will be more about learning and growing in awareness. All growth in awareness leads back to Source. That growth is the expansion of consciousness. You are moving out of the need for more lifetimes and into a new stage of spiritual responsibilities.

Does this mean I'm going to die soon?

No, although that is up to you. You do have a responsibility that you accepted before this birth to bring many souls into higher consciousness and guide them on this side as well as on Earth.

I'm not sure what to do about that.

Stay present. Expand your spiritual energy, and raise your frequency. Ask for guidance. Live in both worlds.

You make it sound so easy.

With practice and trust, it can be as simple and as easy as breathing with the intent to embody Spirit. In your heart, you know it is the only thing worth doing. No, it doesn't preclude having a life. In fact, it is the most vibrant living you can experience.

Breathing with the intent to bridge worlds for just 100 breaths a day, equal to spending just 15 of your minutes in the Unified Field Meditation, will bring you amazing happiness and joy. Imagine what 1,000 breaths could bring you! You can still move around, take action, and live in the moment. But this will create bigger, more momentous moments, moments that are richer, more expansive, and more jam-packed than typical experience.

Then your life becomes like a string of pearls, each moment more lustrous, more self-effulgent, and more entrancing than the next. All this beauty from an irritation in an oyster! Coat your irritations with a celestial frequency to grow your own pearl of great price.

There it was again, the pearl of great price. When I had encountered it before, my guide, Laughter, had brought it down to me from the heavens. It had been a symbol of grace, and at the time, I had experienced that grace as a gift from outside of myself. What a different perspective this was, to consider the pearl as something within me that I was creating through my own process of healing and growth. Clearly I had grown into a new stage of responsibility for my experience on Earth.

Please talk to me about my commitment to guide souls on Earth.

Your leadership, your guidance and example can have a profound effect on those around you. You can elevate people's spirits, help them get unstuck, and move them on to new energetic heights. This is your talent. It is your ability to respond to these types of soul integration requests that makes you who you are.

Having these gifts, it becomes your responsibility to put them to good use. This is not coming from me; it is coming from you and your own agreement with your Higher Self. This time, I am the messenger and you created the message. Do you remember?

I vaguely recall being in a soul group and agreeing to spread the Word. This memory was especially fresh as a child. I always felt that I had known Jesus, and, if I encountered Him again, I promised I would follow Him and help bring His message of love and peace to everyone in the world.

That you did. Only, now you are becoming Him. Once you followed; now you can lead.

I must admit this is making me squirm. Not only do I not feel like Jesus, I also don't have a single person who is interested in following these conversations.

OK, try this on for size. You are a glorious, luminous, divine being who has the power to bring souls into the Light of God.

Hmmm... I feel a paradox coming on.

So true. You are who you think you are, and also so much more. Raise your vibration, and not only will you walk hand-in-hand with Jesus, you will be indistinguishable from him. Even you will not know the difference, or put positively, you will know you are the One.

Let's walk it back a step. I thought you said I was becoming Him. How is that? In what way? I feel like a schmuck, not the Savior.

The process you are in is the same one that made Jesus the Christ, which transformed the man into his true Godhood. That was the whole point of the exercise Jesus took upon himself when he incarnated.

He came to Earth through birth, just like everyone else. He was born with his consciousness veiled and undertook the challenge of regaining his full connection to Spirit. He broke through his human resistance and carried out his divine mission, showing everyone that it could be done. Jesus the Christ stands as a leader among Spirit, inspiring all souls in their journey back to God.

OK, this feels better. You're saying I am becoming more Christ-like as I raise my vibration.

Hmmm... I'm sensing resistance coming on.

You refuse to believe you could be just like Jesus, when that is the very reason He came to Earth and set an example of what is possible for every human, including you. You don't want the perceived responsibility of being a fully Enlightened Master.

Actually, living on a level with the Masters is an exquisite freedom and sublime joy. Master souls have the ability to respond to any and all challenges. Each moment is eternal. Gratitude for the gifts of God simply exudes out of their radiant bodies. Masters are separate and still One.

It's a good deal, believe me. I wouldn't sell you short!

You're right again, of course. I keep scratching and clawing my way back to a comfortable identity in which I get to make sensible baby steps in consciousness and hide in excuses about my human frailty. What's a guy to do?

Forgive yourself. That is, give yourself the benefit of full trust as if now was before. You had foreknowledge of the pickle you were putting yourself in when you chose to embody. Yet you came anyway. You trusted your Higher Self to complete your mission. And you're doing a fine job of it.

Just take the next step, breathe the next breath, and act out of the moment in full connection with Spirit. There is nothing to live up to, no code to follow, and no place where you must hang your hat. There is no hat!

Simply live in the highest consciousness you can at any given moment. You can't make a mistake. No appointments, no disappointments. No successes, no failures. All consciousness and all love, all the time, even though there is no time.

Give it up for yourself! Let's hear it for you! Give it up, let guilt go, and forgive.

So I let go and lead. This is my soul commitment. I guess this means teaching, healing, and guiding.

Yes, but there's more. For an unlimited time, you can have your own guides teaching, healing, and instructing you. If you call in now, we'll give you two guides for the price of Oneness.

But wait, there's even more! If you forgive yourself in the next 10 moments, you will be absolutely free. Now that's an offer you can't refuse!

Aion, you are the greatest.

No, God is the Greatest!

16

Healing Energy
Leaks

"Healing your energy leaks will get you home."

~ Aion

In the days that followed, Aion continued the healing that had begun in me with the earlier emotional clearing process. Things between my wife and me had not improved, but my own state of mind certainly did. Instruction from Aion on energy amplitude and frequency encouraged me to continue.

Aion, I am amazed at the changes in my life. I feel renewed.

This moment is fresh and new, vibrating with celestial energy. It is both just like all other moments over the eons of consciousness and also unique, another opportunity to know God. It is the same moment we in Spirit have always known.
How are you feeling about being God enough?

I am feeling more whole, less leaky. The clearing you did with me seems to have plugged a big hole in me.

Yes, though it is more of a stitching up the wound so it can heal, rather than a patch. As the raw edges of your energy body fuse, less spiritual energy leaks out. This raises your amplitude and helps raise your vibration.

Could you talk more about the importance of increasing amplitude?

If you think of the energy running through your spiritual body as a stream of water through a hose, the volume of the stream is its amplitude. The amplitude of water pumped through a garden hose is less than that through a fire hose. More amplitude of energy flowing through an energy body means more energy available for the support of higher frequencies and the work of Spirit.

The other part of the equation is frequency. Technically speaking, frequency refers to the number of times per second that the water pulsates or vibrates from being pumped through the hose. Frequency measures how frequently this pulsation happens.

All matter vibrates at the atomic level, marking it with a corresponding characteristic frequency. Even though you can't see it, you can often feel it. Think of the hose again, which you can feel vibrating in your hand as the water moves through it. Or consider an orchestra. High notes from a piccolo produce higher frequencies, while a cello string vibrates at the lower end of the range.

The ideal state for communicating with us is an energy frequency that vibrates fast enough to put you in the present, with enough energy amplitude to supercharge your receptors.

Energetic healing is a process that raises both the amount of energy and the rate of vibration in the client. The person receiving the healing does this, with encouragement from the healer and a little help from our friends in Spirit. The healer helps the client hold the increased charge and pay loving attention to any holes until they heal.

What does a life without leaks look like?

Oh, it's completely boring. No drama-rama. Nothing to look forward to. Certainly there are no vacations because there is nothing to vacate and nothing to run away from. It's just an endless Now of bliss, regardless of circumstances. You'd hate it.

Seriously? I didn't think Spirit would be sarcastic.

We are always having a little fun with you just to keep you interested. The point is, being present is a big change in life, and it is the jumping-off point for a life in Spirit that is almost unimaginable to most people. What might it be like for you?

A symphony of yogurt fruit salad bursting in your mouth. A deep breath that satisfies every immediate need. A look of love and a smile of appreciation for a loved one. Feeling the grief of a friend in pain and touching her heart without missing a beat of your own. An early morning stillness that moves you.

This list could go on and on, but I think you get the picture.

I do. It looks just like what is, in the moment.

Yes, indeed. It is the I Am in the What Is.

I would like to increase my frequency and be a better bridge between worlds. How can I do this?

Improving this capability is a function of practice. You have been living in a higher frequency for a while now, and you can tell the difference, can't you?

I can. I feel amazingly uplifted and wide open, appreciative of my life despite its current difficulties.

As your energy has grown, so has your ability to speak with us. These dialogues not only bring forward information, but also allow us to help heal you by sealing your leaks. When you leak less energy, you have more energy and can experience a higher frequency.

The simple answer to your question about how to increase your frequency is to continue to practice. There is no substitute. You have noticed how important it is to connect with Spirit deeply, every day and periodically throughout the day. It holds your attention and fills you up.

Now it's time to take it up a notch. Practice the Unified Field Meditation we have transmitted each morning before starting your day and again before going to bed. This will accelerate your shift in frequency. Ask us to help, and we will.

Healing and Sealing Leaks

When you are experiencing the flow of energy through your body, use your hands to contact it, amplify it, and gently move it. Use your voice to hum or tone into the areas that feel sluggish or stuck. You can use touch, sounds, and even smells to help you amplify and move your energy. Use all of your senses to help you expand your energy body and increase your frequency.

It is also important to increase the integrity of your container for this energy. The container is your energy field, which grows stronger and bigger as you unify it. Within the energy field are what you might call energy bodies, which are interpenetrating layers of fields, each with its own edge or membrane and unique range of frequencies.

Each chakra energy center also has its own field that contacts the fields of the chakras above and below it. The chakras, when properly functioning and balanced, provide a smooth flow of energy through the body. They comprise one integrated layer of energy with its own energetic membrane. All the chakras working in harmony provide an excellent foundation for a unified field.

The physical body, with its organs and systems of electromagnetic, chemical, and biological processes, is another layer with its own field.

A primary layer at the edge of your field surrounds all of this. For health, this surface must be intact, smooth, and without leaks. Even slow leaks reduce the amount of energy available for increasing frequency. The outer edge of this field encapsulates your entire being, body and soul.

Without making this too complicated, the point is to heal any leaks that allow energy to escape from your energy bodies or from the outer edge of your field.

How do I recognize leaks?

You can recognize them as sensations in your body. When you scan your energy bodies with your hands, you can feel the leaks as anomalies in your field. They may feel hot, cold, rough, lumpy, or even prickly. The membrane of the field may feel soft, or you may even feel a hole in it. The soft spots may be semi-permeable when they should be sealed tight.

You will note that radiation in the forms of light and heat naturally escapes through these membranes. This is as it should be. However, this typically should happen at the same rate throughout the sphere-shaped membrane of the energy body. If more light or heat is escaping from one part than another, this is a sign of an energy imbalance within the system.

When your energy field expands, it should do so at the same pace throughout. If one portion expands and another does not, this is a sign of stuck or congested energy, or perhaps some leakage.

Available energy is never lacking. The only question is, how much energy can you radiate in a continuous flow in all directions? This is why healing your leaks and increasing your ability to bring our energy and messages through clearly is so important. Healing your energy leaks will get you home.

Those tingles that you are feeling as you bring the energy up from your feet, through your base chakra, through the heart, and to the top of your head indicate that you are raising your frequency. Learn to raise the energy independently of your breathing.

Cycle the energy up the back of the spine to the top of the head and then down the front of the spine to the feet. You can stop anywhere along this grand loop of energy to dissolve pain, energize congested areas, and clear new pathways for the flow. If you get distracted or lose your focus, simply stop, breathe, and begin again.

Pay attention to your energy throughout the day. Learn to cycle it, move it, and expand it as you move from moment to moment. This way, you can live in the flow.

As my energy expanded, I still found myself fumbling through my human limitations. Fortunately, Aion continued to instruct me in how to recognize and move past these limits for greater connection with my soul.

Aion, I was unable to get an early start this morning. On top of that, I've had to troubleshoot a software problem. I apologize for the delay.

Stevie, no need to worry about the delay. We are always with you. However, you are not always with us. Your frustration and tension during the troubleshooting makes it difficult for us to get through to you.

Try some deep breathing and relaxation exercises from time to time when you notice yourself tensing up. This will give you better reception and allow us to feed ideas for potential solutions to you. We are an endless source of ideas, and you would do well to take advantage of this.

Remember, not every plan you make for your day will work out as you thought it would. Grace, serendipity, and our intervention will all help your day unfold beneficially if that is your request. Just remember to ask.

When the details of daily life seem to be mounting up, choose to take the time to practice modulating your energy and unifying your field to shift your frequency. You will be glad you did.

What can I do when I feel my energy frequency dropping during my day, but I can't take time at that moment to move into a full-blown meditation?

Practice for Raising Frequency

Take three deep breaths, in through the nose, exhaling through the mouth, and mentally ask us for help to bring your vibration back up to your desired frequency. Know that we always hear, love, and support you.

It's not like you have to do mental gymnastics to reach us. A simple request will do. We may pour energy in through your crown chakra at the top of your head, pouring in golden white light that will fill up your energy body to help shift your state.

And you can help yourself. You can scan your energy body by visualizing it, noticing any abnormalities like leaking, overheating, or bulging. Look for a sticky emotion, a painful feeling in your body or congested energy, and breathe light into that spot to dissolve the blockage. By realigning your energy centers and breathing into them, one by one, you can reestablish the frequency level you desire.

Your feelings will guide you, and you can always check with us to see if you are sensing the area correctly. Then work energetically with that area until it is sealed, soothed, and healed, back to its natural state. With practice, this will come easily.

I am so grateful for your guidance. I feel I am embarking on a new journey with you guiding me, healing me, and bringing the best parts of me forward. I can barely imagine how my life will unfold from here.

As you continue to practice, you will grow. Many new dimensions and insights will open for you. You have every reason to believe you can achieve all that you can imagine in the world of Spirit, which is everywhere.

I notice that you still sometimes make a distinction between the world of Spirit and your world. I want to emphasize that this is old thinking. When the time comes that you can move effortlessly between worlds—but without moving, and in no time at all—you will see that there is no distinction.

Aion, I just want to serve you.

Serve yourself, and you will be serving us. Serve us, and you serve God. Again, these distinctions will blur and then disappear when you are more able to navigate with your intention and your energy.

As you have said, you still need to wake up every day and put one foot in front of the other as you walk the path of human life. But being human does not preclude being completely in Spirit either.

The multiverse and all its inhabitants are in support of your continued development and are looking forward to seeing you on this side more often. Simply follow the path as it appears before you, knowing we walk at your side.

17

Reincarnation and Karma

"There is much to appreciate and enjoy in a human
life. The trick is to let go of identification
with all this goodness."

~ Aion

I'd like to talk about reincarnation. You mentioned before that it was my decision whether or not to reincarnate. How? Why would I ever choose to reincarnate?

The relief upon returning to Spirit is only matched by the desire to return again to Earth. Earth's magnificence, the beauty of canyons and mountains, oceans, forests, lakes and rivers, the spreading plains, sunsets and sunrises, has a huge allure for those in Spirit. Experiencing the physical senses, the joys and challenges of life, and getting to know consciousness in a human body are all a huge draw toward experiencing another lifetime.

Then there is your soul group, with connections and promises made and broken. So much love exists between souls who have experienced earth lifetimes together that they willingly give up their place in Spirit to assist each other on the Earth path.

There is no judgment if a spirit decides not to reincarnate, for there is much to do on our side of the veil as well. It is for each soul to decide. As you know, each soul has a panel of guides and celestial beings that help that soul make the best choices for the next stage of development.

Souls are often anxious for their spirit guides to tell them what to do, which is, of course, not the way of Spirit. Guides give hints and make suggestions when asked, but it is up to each individual soul to choose whether or not they will follow those suggestions. Souls have free will and the ultimate responsibility for choosing the path back to God.

When you shared before that the choice to reincarnate was mine on many levels, what levels were you speaking of?

These levels may be a bit difficult for you to understand. They are actually not hierarchical levels or even planes of consciousness. They exist holistically in multiple dimensions.

For the sake of this discussion, we will say that your Higher Self, the highest fragment of your soul that is closest to Source, plays as much a part in the decision as that part of you now on the earth plane. When you leave the earth plane and visit us here in Spirit, you experience our side of the veil from another kind of body. With that body, known as the causal body, you do the work of forwarding your development on this side of the veil as you do in your physical body on Earth. It plays a part in the decision to take a human form as well.

So all the aspects of you, along with your counsel of guides, your angels, the archangels, and Source work together to choose the appropriate next place or plane for your consciousness to grow best.

What do you think you would gain and what do you feel you would lose by passing through the veil without returning to Earth again? I know this is a difficult question to ask because you are not entirely conscious of all the opportunities available on different planes, but you understand enough, even now, living on the earth plane, to discuss it.

I am so moved by Earth's physical beauty and majesty, its complexity and diversity of life. I experience great love for my family, friends, and the community that surrounds me.

Yes, I am attached to the physical body. I delight in being alive, eating, danc-ing, loving, and the simple warmth of the sun on my skin. I love the discovery of each new day and the learning that comes from being present in the Earth's environment.

There is much to appreciate and enjoy in a human life. The trick is to let go of identification with all this goodness. Instead, be who you are in the highest vibration of your soul. Be on Earth and live in Spirit. Everything that you love so much about a human life is avail-able to you in Spirit as well.

As for evolving, who do you think created the diversity of life on the planet? Did you think that genetics was an accident? Did you imagine that life's resilience was left to chance?

Life reflects the creation and creativity of Spirit. Many in Spirit attend to the development of Earth and all its species. Evolving and creating unfolds constantly in Spirit.

You believe that leaving the body means leaving Earth and all its beauty. Consider that by learning to live in both worlds, you not only create the option of Heaven on Earth now, you also create the possibility of remaining connected to Earth from Heaven later. In other words, when you leave your physical body behind, you will have the option to stay with us in Spirit on this side of the veil, con-tinue your return to the Godhead, and still pursue your interests, including guiding those souls still on Earth. As a Soul Guardian, the opportunities open to you are limitless. You can renew your work as a soul pilot, supporting new galaxies in their emerging con-sciousness, or do anything you choose.

I feel like I'm being recruited here.

The choice is yours, of course. But you have already passed the test of entry and are welcome at any time to come work with us in the great evolutionary plan. When you learned to accelerate your vibration and pass through the veil to the next frequency, you dem-onstrated the consciousness needed to do the work of Spirit on our side. Consciousness and intent are all that are required.

This is not beyond you; it is what you already are. In the body or not, you will still be practicing, learning, and growing in awareness. Consciousness is a practice. All beings are learning as they go, doing their best, which is all that is required to take them home. The understanding and resources of the soul are vast, beyond time and place.

Don't you mean, "time and space?"

No. The ego is dependent on time and place as identifiers, convincers for a linear reality. Memories are very much linked to locations, manners of dress, and defining events of a time period. This is why past life memories often emerge when visiting a new place or seeing the footwear or clothing from the period.

I knew Aion was addressing my own experience directly with these words. On my first visit to the Coliseum in Rome, I walked into its playing field through a tunnel once used by chariots. As I passed through the tunnel, I looked down at the deep grooves in the stone made by the wheels of thousands of chariots, and suddenly I found myself transported. My feet were in rope sandals, the hem of my burlap tunic was tattered and torn, and my hands were tied behind my back. I looked down again at the grooves in the stone and was surprised to see that they were suddenly much shallower than they had been when I was looking at them just an instant before.

I looked up at my friends and said, "The last time I was here, these grooves were much shallower." Of course, they looked back at me completely perplexed. In this lifetime, I had never been to the Coliseum, something they all knew before we entered. But I was re-experiencing my lifetime as an early Christian, when I had been martyred there.

Another experience came in India. When I first arrived at my guru's ashram and ran to the top of a sandy hill, I looked down and saw that my feet, which had been boot-clad only a moment before, were suddenly brown and bare. Looking back up, I caught a glimpse of a river flowing past.

"I'm back, I'm back!" I thought gleefully. "It's the holy river, and I've been gone so long!" Until that moment, I had no idea that my guru's ashram in Hardwar was on the famous Ganges River. But now I was remembering my life as an Indian sadhu, when the Ganges had been both my home and the center of my spiritual life.

Another vivid past-life remembrance happened when I visited the Brooklyn Museum with a friend. We walked into a room full of Native American clothing and artifacts displayed in large glass cases, each about 4 feet by 6 feet. Upon stepping into the room, I was inexplicably pulled to a case about 20 feet away that held a mannequin dressed in an intricately beaded deerskin coat.

"Hey, that's my coat!" I told my friend, who still stood back at the room's entrance. For me, it wasn't like having a distant memory—more like stumbling upon something that I used to wear often but had inadvertently misplaced only a few years ago.

To my right, I saw a similar case full of all kinds of different Native American footwear. Again, without reading any of the placards attached to each object, I went straight for a pair of moccasins at the end of the case. Standing in front of them, I told my friend, "These are my shoes!"

Without thinking, I had spoken about both pieces of clothing in the present tense. I was experiencing a powerful sense of déjà vu, my mind flooding with memories of the woman who had beaded the coat and shoes for me, my wife in that lifetime.

When my friend and I took the time to read the museum's comments about each piece of clothing, we discovered that the coat and shoes had indeed belonged to one person, the chief of a New England tribe. I knew without any prompting that the tribe had lived in long houses because I was remembering them. The energy of this experience was so intense for me that we left the museum without looking at anything else.

Aion, I see so many identifications!

The Parting of the Red Sea, The Council of Nicaea, the eruption of Mt. Vesuvius, your birthday, and all kinds of anniversaries and remembrances serve to anchor the ego's sense of importance, its own reality. The progression and succession of dramatic changes reinforces the illusion of linearity. Ego mind uses history as proof of its concept that life is a painful plodding from event to event, accreting small grains of knowledge as a clam makes a pearl around an irritating grain of sand.

This is just not how it is when the ego lets go to the free flow of divine energy. Suddenly, life is a river of joy, and the soul naturally flows with that celestial current.

All the resources of your soul and of all beings are available to you when you enter into soul knowing. Deep soul knowing springs out of being in the moment. It is not that suddenly everything in your life works perfectly and all desires manifest. It is just that whatever is happening doesn't take you out of the flow.

Your unified field, as an integrated energy system, can metabolize and transmute any experience into divine energy, dissolving pain and separation. You are one with life and Spirit. Time and place are no longer a consideration. You have no preferences and no references. You are not this and not that. You simply are.

This is the freedom, the wholeness you long for; this is speaking with One Voice. This is the song your soul sings and the wings on which it flies back to Source.

What about unfinished business from my past lives? Is there anything I'm supposed to do about completing them, tying up those karmic loose ends?

As I typed this question, I clearly heard Aion chuckling. I had a hunch that Aion's warm, appreciative laughter rose in response to the naiveté of my question.

I admire your sense of responsibility, my son. But the truth is, those lives have been continuing to unfold with other versions of you in other dimensions. In those other dimensions, they are being completed, the loose threads woven into a larger tapestry.

You continue that process in this timeframe and are free to bless those other lifetimes and move forward, working the threads of your new life into the grand tapestry. What matters is only what matters to you. It is your consciousness that gives your experience meaning, if you know what I mean. Shift your consciousness, and what matters to you most will immediately have a different meaning.

You are free to be. There are no shackles to the past except those of your own making. Your futures are not set. You make them as well. From this present moment, all things are possible. Unlimited life is yours for the asking. Ask for that now, and it shall be granted unto you.

Thank you, Aion, I want to experience that unlimited life in Spirit. I am so moved and so thankful for your gifts. What can I do for you?

You know what. Practice living in both worlds. Be your true Self, your Higher Self, and find your way back to God-ness.

18

Family Matters

"Love brings freedom, both for the one giving and
the one receiving."

~ Aion

When my daughter was only in the fifth grade, she had a seizure
at school. Since then, seizures had dominated and even sometimes threatened her life. But she had eventually found a way to live
with this challenge, becoming both a mother and a successful lawyer.

With this history, her birthdays always felt important to me. Now,
as another birthday came, I was reflecting again on our life together.
Because I was working with Aion, I hoped for answers to questions I
had been carrying for decades.

When she was still in high school, my daughter had hated taking
her medication. Because she could remember nothing afterwards, a
seizure felt to her like little more than a really good nap. From her perspective, taking her medication meant defeat. Even though the medication fully managed her condition, taking it felt to her like admitting
something about her was different or wrong. Her compliance with
treatment was spotty at best.

During this time, I had been jogging down a rocky dirt road, when
a vivid image flashed through my mind of her white-knuckled hands
locked on her steering wheel. In the vision that followed, I found myself looking out of her eyes, in full color and 3-D. For a moment, I be-

came her. I could feel her paralysis and fear, her inability to steer her car as a seizure overtook her body. As the scene unfolded in this vision, I helplessly watched through her eyes as her car begin to drift over the double line, directly into an oncoming vehicle.

The images took my breath away with their clarity and reality. I felt as if my heart had stopped, and I had to quit jogging. As I did, the vision faded.

I shook my head. "I'm just imagining things," I told myself.

I started jogging again, and as I entered a clearing in the woods, I experienced the vision a second time, even more powerfully than the first. I stopped short in my tracks and practically fell down.

Peering into a crystal blue sky, I shouted, "God, I don't pray very often, I know. But I work for you. I do my best to carry your work forward on Earth, and I promise to continue to do your work throughout my life. So I beg you now, please, please spare my daughter from this. Whatever it takes, please, for my sake, protect her from this harm. Give her pain to me."

For an instant, the forest stood silent. Birds flew by noiselessly overhead. Shafts of light pierced the canopy, illuminating the ground around me in dappled pools. Time stopped.

Then the wind rustled suddenly through the leaves, and the sound of the stream next to the road filled my ears again, cascading loudly over the stones. The spell was broken.

Deep inside, my anxiety melted. I felt heard by God.

A huge sense of relief washed over me as I wiped a few tears from my cheek and began running again. Reaching the end of the rocky road, I turned around to return home the way I had come. When I reached the clearing again where I had prayed, I stepped on a small stone.

As I did, I felt my ankle roll over to the outside of my foot. I could hear the ligaments in it tear, and I went down in a heap. For my work as a consultant, I was on the opposite coast of the country from where I lived and still had a full day of consulting to do the next day. I couldn't afford to stop for this. Cursing my bad luck, I hobbled over to the stream and put my foot, shoe and all, into the cold running water.

Sitting on a stone at the edge of the stream, I watched my ankle swell to twice its normal size, spilling over the upper edge of my shoe. If I took the shoe off, I would never get it back on again.

Looking back, I must have been in shock since I completely forgot the vision I had experienced only minutes before, including my urgent request to God. I got up unsteadily and hobbled the mile and a half back to the lodge without a single thought about my premonition. I could not even remember to warn my daughter.

This was three days before her accident.

The morning before it happened, my daughter was leaving for school from a friend's house. She heard a voice as she got into her car telling her, "Let your friend drive."

Of course, she shrugged it off. But as she turned the key in the car door, she heard it again, more forcefully: "Let your friend drive." She refused and got behind the wheel.

Driving down a high-speed, two-lane road, she had a seizure. Her friend later told me that my daughter's hands gripped the steering wheel as she seized, the car slowly drifting left over the double line at 40 miles per hour, directly into an oncoming car.

Then suddenly, her car moved back to the right, across the lane in the other direction. She crashed into a parked car that surged forward into the next parked car and then the next, totaling all three parked cars and her own.

Getting that call from the hospital was one of the worst moments of my life. But my daughter walked away with only a minor concussion, bumps, and bruises. Her friend was uninjured, and no one else was involved.

As happens after a seizure, my daughter had no memory of the accident. A day later, I took her to the junkyard to see her wrecked car, hoping to impress upon her the seriousness of taking her medication.

Only then did I suddenly remember my technicolor vision in the woods. Shaking, I told her what had happened. Then she remembered being told by a voice not to drive the car. Later, after interviewing her friend, I put the pieces together.

The memory of the accident was vivid for me as I connected with Aion about my current concerns for her.

Today is my daughter's birthday, and my heart goes out to her for the struggles and challenges she currently faces in her life.

Your child has her own life and her own children, and you must let her go her own way. Of course, sending her light and love supports her inner work, but you know it is impossible and even unfair to emotionally take on her challenges.

What do you mean, unfair?

We mean that she, just like all souls, exists to become more conscious on the path back to Source. Taking on the emotional, spiritual, and psychic challenges of your children simply delays their development. When she was in school, you wouldn't do her homework for her, would you?

Parents must walk a fine line between supporting and enabling, helping children avoid lessons that can't be assimilated by a child but allowing those that can. This helps the child grow into awareness incrementally. It can feel like heartbreak to a parent, but it teaches non-attachment for the parent and maturity for the child.

Your daughter has her own path to clear, and she is walking on it. If it pains you to see her struggles, you are still trying to take on her lessons as you did prior to her car crash. You received the requested intervention at that time because of your deep, everlasting love for your daughter and your strong connection to Source.

Why couldn't I remember and warn her?

She was a teenager then and not yet fully awake. We warned her twice not to drive, but she didn't listen.

Your impassioned plea led to a sprained ankle for you, but reduced her bodily damage to relatively minor injury instead of a major one or death in a head-on collision. That head-on crash would have occurred during her seizure, except for your premonition and your petition to God and her Higher Self.

Your plea also spared other drivers on the road. Many others would have been impacted by the aftermath of the crash.

Naturally, she didn't want to have to take medication for the rest of her life. Her condition made her feel abnormal. She just wanted to be a normal teenager but knew this would never be. So she denied it.

A wake-up call in the form of the accident was her decision. Her Higher Self responded to your plea but did not allow you to take her lesson away so that she would still have to face her denial about the seizures. God and her Higher Self intervened so the two of you could make a new agreement to change her decision.

She lived. Now your daughter is facing another call to consciousness, and it is up to her to open to it or not. You can't psychically carry her on your back anymore as you did when she was a child. She has chosen the path upon which she walks, and that is only as it could be.

Stevie, you can forgive yourself now for not warning your daughter about the accident. Had you remembered to warn her, she might have missed her opportunity to wake up. It simply was not up to you. Her Higher Self took that responsibility from you for her own growth.

Thank you, Aion. I am moved to tears. This is truly amazing. All this time, I blamed myself. I was sure that God controlled the outcome of the accident, and I had somehow failed.

Those beliefs are relics of your religious upbringing. Now you understand the real deal and can let them go.

Only you control the flow of your life stream. The path of that flow reflects your consciousness. The flow of being moves through many forks and eddies in the river of life. Your Higher Self guides the sequence of events, realizations, and seeming coincidences that you encounter as the waves of your consciousness flow downstream to merge with the sea of All.

Stop swimming against the current; stay in the present and go with the flow, my son. Surf the waves of your highest frequencies and enjoy the ride! After all, this life is a gift you gave to yourself.

Just 10 days later, my sister had her birthday.

Aion, because today is my sister's birthday, I'm wondering about family connections in Spirit.

We are all connected, as you know, but many souls belong to a larger soul group who look after each other and help each other develop on the journey back to Source. These connections are real, though often unrecognized while a soul is in a body.

Many times, people in your family are part of your soul group. Whether they are with you on Earth or still in Spirit, they make it part of their development to help you with yours. This is part of the divine plan to ensure every soul has all the resources it requires while continuing on its path back to Source.

As you know, not all of these relationships seem healthy or even helpful, though some are productive and supportive. This is as the souls agreed it would be. All the same rules apply to soul group members as to any person you encounter in your lifetime. Appreciating others, helping when you can, and sending light and love when you can't take action is the road to liberation.

Love brings freedom, both for the one giving and the one receiving. Freedom is a big issue for you, is it not?

You're right about that. In my heart, I have always longed to be free, even though I don't think I have really understood, until recently, what real freedom looks like.

Yes, a very insightful comment on your part. There is hope for you yet.

Seriously, though, it is very good that you understand that freedom comes from the inside and not from the circumstances of your life on the outside, in the material world. When we speak of the material, we aren't talking about income or status. We mean the world of so-called "real" substance around you. That material world, though not to be ignored, will never give you the freedom you desire.

True freedom resides in the moment. Not before the moment and not after the moment, only in this very moment. True freedom is timeless, the direct experience of timelessness, one of my favorite topics. One question to ask is, "Who am I outside of time?"

When you can answer this question in the moment from a place of full knowingness, then you are free. Free of your stories, your history, your past lives, and all the fears, "real" or imagined, none of which define you.

Remembering who you really are in the moment brings peace and freedom. Peace, because in realizing the truth of your being, you experience your divine nature. Freedom, because you are simply consciousness.

Some have called this enlightenment, nirvana, ascension, or realization, and all are correct to a degree. But it is not a state you can attain, not something to acquire. It is simply the I Am.

It seems to me that all emotional work, self-development, and learning in a lifetime pale in comparison to the skill of being present in the moment.

Presence is the key to life, death, and life beyond life and death. True life, at any level of vibration, is lived in the moment. You might say it could be lived in multiple moments within each moment, but it is still just a single moment of presence, even when you are choosing which strand of reality to follow in that moment.

The moment, this very moment, holds unshakable freedom because it is the point where you can know the full expanse of your soul's connectedness across the multiverse. This is a joy beyond understanding. It puts your life and all of existence into proper perspective.

So you want to be free? Then be present!

Where is the flavor, where is the personality of each soul, and how does the I Am state reflect that?

This is an example of linear thinking, my son. The "you" who thinks you are your personality actually has a much bigger identity in the multiverse. Yes, there is still an identity, called the monad, which is the individual essence, the unique frequency of your soul.

Each soul is separate and still part of the One. The human identity you call Stevie is but a mere reflection of your divinity.

Another question to ask is, "Who am I if I am not Stevie?" If you strip away all of your Stevie-ness, who remains? And indeed, there is still a consciousness to perceive all that is not-Stevie.

This is another aspect of freedom. True freedom is being unencumbered by a limited identity. Experiencing limitlessness leaves human understanding in the dust, the very same dust to which your body returns after death, while the soul lives on, immortal. This is one of the few teachings that conventional religions have gotten correct.

What they don't understand, however, is how to help people achieve this state. That has been a dismal failure. Following religious laws, codes, and commandments may help society function more smoothly, more humanely, but does little to actually raise a person's consciousness in the moment. Outside of a very few temples, churches, mosques, and monasteries that teach and practice the highest spiritual truths, most organized religions seed and cultivate a state of mind that sends people down a track that inevitably leads to more lifetimes.

So, young soul—and I only mean that in relation to my agelessness—if you want to be free and help your family and your soul group, live in the moment. Only this moment counts. Source lives in the moment, and you will always find Spirit here.

19

Becoming an Apprentice

"All healing modalities, all techniques come down
to this: Love heals."

~ Aion

Early on, Aion instructed me to go out, buy a massage table, and invite friends over to lie down on it. Of course, I was flabbergasted. Even though I already had many years under my belt as a Gestalt psychotherapist and a hypnotherapist, I had very little experience or training in energy healing. But the message was clear: I would receive all the help and instruction I needed from Aion and The Beings of Light. Reluctantly at first, and then with growing confidence, I began to give energy healing sessions from our home.

Fairly quickly I developed a training process with Aion. Before a session, I would sit down with my laptop for guidance and instruction. Afterwards, I would repeat the process, asking Aion for feedback.

The guidance I received during these before-and-after conversations with Aion was both encouraging and direct. My team gave detailed instruction on things like timing, speech, body movement, and breath, as well as my ability to track and read the input of my client's guides. Without realizing it, I had become an apprentice.

I would love to discuss the healing session I have coming up tomorrow. How should I begin, and what should I do? What kinds of treatments should I incorporate into the session?

In your healing work, begin by breathing together with your client, which will raise and synchronize your frequencies. Ask us to help and we will. We are on your team and will guide you and your client to a new awareness in higher energy levels.

Know that it is not you alone doing the healing. It is quite all right to simply find your way with our help, moment-to-moment during the session, without a prearranged plan. This allows us to move you and the client together.

As the session unfolds, it will become obvious where energy is stuck, congested, or weak and needs our help to flow smoothly. I suggest that you speak to the client, sharing your perceptions as they arise. If you are so moved, pass instructions from us to the client to help smooth out the process.

Your energy added to ours, your client's, and her guides' will work synergistically to elevate her frequency, and results will come easily. Remember, you don't have to try too hard. Simply relax and allow the session to unfold.

At the beginning of a session, please remember to ask the client to request the healing. It may be as simple as asking, "What healing do you request today?" Be sure to explain that the session will take its own unique course. Share that we are all on the same team, and the client can continue the work we begin together on her own at any time.

You may feel moved to include a variety of modalities and to work on the various energy centers to increase and integrate the flow of energy throughout the client's light body. Go with the flow! Work with it, and continuously describe what you are sensing and doing. Ask the client to participate.

Also, continually breathe together. You may stop from time to time to get re-synchronized with the client and reconnect with us if necessary. Her guides will be present as well, and we may be relaying information to you from them to pass along to her. You do not need to understand these messages yourself. These are simply for the client, and it may take her some time to understand those messages.

Remember to use your hands to sense energy. Touch, move, or amplify it as you feel called to do so. You can use your voice for the same purpose. Another option is to look into the client's eyes to transmit energy and help her focus on increasing her rate of vibration.

If the client has emotions welling up that need expression, stop and take the time to allow their release. When you ask for our intervention, these releases will be less painful and shorter in duration, resulting in a more powerful healing than otherwise might have been possible. Once the release of emotional energy has wound down, breathe together, and finish the session. It may take several sessions for complete healing on any particular issue or blockage to the flow of higher frequency.

See these sessions as a dance, with many beings synchronized and moving together to a celestial harmony, effortlessly matching each other's movements.

Suddenly I remembered learning to square dance in the fifth grade.

No, not a square dance but a circle dance. In the circle are spirits, linked arm-in-arm with you, with the client, and with us. Outside, around that circle, is a larger circle of angelic hosts contributing their energy to the transformation and healing that the client requested.

At the close of the session, have your client stand and bend her knees to the ground and reorient herself to her body. While doing this, help her maintain the newly created connection with Spirit and her guides, supporting her to live both in Heaven and on Earth.

Small steps are fine. The healings will progress at a natural pace. For some, simply being in the Now moment is healing enough. Every session does not have to be something to write home about. Each healing is but a step toward the next. As energy leaks are sealed, the flow of energy and the client's frequency increase. With this, she will have more ability to clear blockages for herself.

Of course, all options are open for full and complete healings in any moment. Just do not let your needs or expectations drive the process. This is not about you looking good. It is not even about you knowing what you are doing, since we and your client's guides are doing it with you. Rest assured. Everything will proceed as it should and only as it could.

At the end of the session, you and the client may want to sit down and discuss what happened. The client may wish to take some notes to identify a thread or a theme for the next session.

We sense your anxiety. Don't worry. We are sending you love and confidence. Confidence means acting out of the moment with faith that the most appropriate healing is taking place.

You are a brave soul undertaking this journey, and we salute you. Simply pay attention. By staying focused and connected to us, you will know that as you move from moment to moment, we are indeed with you, helping you reawaken to the full realization of Source. If you think you have made a misstep, you have not. Relax and refocus. Our guidance, together with your intuition and empathy, will show you the way.

Learning to apply Aion's teachings definitely took practice. At the end of a session, I sat down with my laptop to ask Aion for feedback.

Thank you so much, Aion, for your guidance in today's healing session with my client. It is wonderful and amazing to feel the client's energies moving, leaks healing, and energy reaching new frequencies.

You are beginning to see Spirit move through you. This is made possible by the grace of God for all those who seek healing for themselves and others. Don't let it go to your head! Stay in your heart as you did today. The healing that the client seeks will always trigger the appropriate energy for their unique situation. Simply allow the energy to flow through, and Spirit will do all the healing that can be done as your client requests and allows.

Do you have any other feedback for me?

Do you really want to hear it?

Yes, I do.

Do even less.

Know that there is really nothing for you to do. Your instincts in the session are very good, but it is best to wait for our lead, especially when moving from one stage of the session to the next. Hold less concern for the outcome of your session by accepting our reassurances that Spirit will prevail. As long as the client allows it, healing will happen.

In this case, the energy you were transmitting came in three distinct waves. For the first two, you were in synch with us. The third one was a bit out of synch because you were rushing ahead of the client's ability to assimilate the powerful transformation she had just gone through. You did catch yourself and pull back, and it was of no consequence to the client. Just be aware of the timing as you proceed.

If you find yourself feeling tired or de-energized, then you have used too much of your own energy in the healing. Simply enter the process as an act of discovery, both for you and your client. Aim to strike a balance between coming from the moment, working with us, and allowing the client to contribute. In the sweet spot, you will feel energized and fully alive at the end of the session. When you heal others, you heal yourself.

The main thing to remember is that we are working with you and through you to make the healing a reality. This is an energy healing that comes from Spirit by the grace of God for the client's highest soul purposes.

Your primary job is expressing our love for the client. These sessions are transforming because of that love energy. For some clients, just finally feeling loved is enough to break the dams holding their energy back. For others, combining that love with intellectual realization and emotional reconnection to lost parts of themselves will get the stream of consciousness flowing again as it should.

The soul healing process doesn't have to take a long time anymore; our dispensation has seen to that. Healing only requires recognition, acknowledgement, and letting go. Everyone proceeds at his or her own pace, and yet healing can occur in an instant with our support.

Healing is always a relief, but clients will also benefit by recognizing that there are more layers of the soul to uncover, more aspects to own and recover, until bliss is the normal state of being.

How best can I express the love Spirit has for each client?

You are doing it. As you contact the client with a loving touch, word, or gaze, or even by breathing with him or her, you feel our unconditional love for that soul. You experience loving them as we do, just as they are. This is why letting go of an agenda for the session is so important. Love moves energy and releases the divine healing flow.

All healing modalities, all techniques come down to this: Love heals. The energy of Spirit that flows through you and each person is love. It is creativity at its finest, the stuff of the multiverse. All of creation arises from love. It can take any shape and transform the formless. But you can't grasp it with the mind. You have to experience it. There is nothing to do but bask in the fine golden mist of love that surrounds you and all sentient beings.

Is there an end to healing?

No, all beings on the path back to Source are healing and continually learning to express higher energies, a process that takes many forms in Spirit. There is always a new consciousness to nurture and a higher love to radiate throughout the multiverse.

You could say that merging with Source is the final healing, the final transformation. But even when a drop of water merges with the ocean, that ocean still contains the single drop. The vast sea can never dilute its individual beingness. In the same way, the original spark of each soul expressed from Source never goes out. Such is the mystery of divine expression.

As you practice, your sessions will go more quickly. You will have a better sense of how the healings are developing, but you will always be operating out of the moment. New and wonderful harmonics will emerge from these healings.

What do you mean by "new and wonderful harmonics?"

As your frequency rises, it generates a new series of tones. You can think of them as a chord of tones and overtones, resonating in your energetic field. Those harmonics move outward, vibrating through the fields of all beings.

This is the game we are playing, the song we are singing, all across the multiverse. We are building a resonant, harmonic chord of love, a song that echoes across galaxies, building upon itself, uplifting all beings as its beautiful tones resonate through their energy fields. Your energy adds harmonics or overtones to this choir. Those overtones resonate, increasing the frequency of everything they touch.

In the past, you have felt alone. But you are not alone. Of course, you never were. This was just your fear. So fear not, my young apprentice. Simply move confidently from moment to moment with faith in your Spirit team and a song of love in your heart. Share that love with every being you encounter, and you will be living in your purpose on purpose.

20

Chakra Balancing

"Being brilliant is more than being bright.
Brilliance in your life and work is the
fruit of spiritual awakening."

~ Aion

Nestled into one of my favorite neighborhoods in town, our house had been my address for more years than I had even known my wife. In it, I had built a successful business, then struggled through a failing one. I had hosted dance parties and wine tastings, events that drew hundreds of people. My wife and I had hosted divine guidance classes from the house that had changed the lives of our students. Sixteen years in it had made it my home.

Still, I understood all too well the financial realities that faced us. I was paying our mortgage out of my retirement savings, a situation I had created by choosing not to go back to work yet. Somehow, sometime, something would have to give.

I know my wife felt hurt and disappointed. And I felt confused. After all, wasn't I following the call of my own soul? How could I walk away now? I was too new in this experience, too tender to go back to high-pressure, high-stress corporate consulting work. If I did, I knew I would likely abandon the task of living in both worlds all over again. On that day back in April when I first picked up my computer with a single question in mind, I never in a million years would have dreamed that my life would unfold like this.

More than once, a part of me considered going back into corporate consulting, even with its crushing stress, to handle the escalating demands of the material world. In my own mind, I had every reason to do so, and most people would have said it was the right thing, given the circumstances. But Aion kept encouraging me, supporting me to go further into my work with healing. Again and again, the message from Aion and The Beings of Light was for me to continue working with them to develop my capacity and fulfill my purpose of bridging Heaven and Earth.

The day I purchased the URL that I would use to sell the house was a grim one.

Aion, I feel like I am not progressing well toward living in both worlds. I can sense a door between worlds opening when I meditate, and my frequency rises, but I'm not passing through to the other side.

This is because your energy has shifted to a higher vibration. You are noticing disturbances in your sleeping patterns and many moments of awareness throughout the day, are you not?

I am. My sleep has been restless and unsatisfying.

These are signs of advancement in containing energy and increasing frequency. Don't worry. As you become accustomed to these new levels, sound sleep will return. The uplifting energy you are experiencing is coming in stages to avoid overwhelming the nervous system.

Be patient and stay with the process in each moment. As your capacity grows, you will learn to modulate your frequency to move freely through dimensions. It takes some practice to refine the ability to navigate and arrive at your desired destination in a conscious state. Remember, not only was Rome not built in a day, but also reality is still under construction, as are you.

Remember, home is where the OM is. Use the frequency of OM to reconnect and recharge. This frequency brings you to the Sacred Now, which is your true Home.

Keep practicing. Your ability to stay focused on the ends will create the means for your conscious arrival on our side of the veil.

I will keep practicing moving energy and increasing my frequency. What else should I practice?

Be sure to look within for leaks at all levels in your energy field. Take a few moments each day to identify specific holes and heal them as we previously discussed. These healings, along with chakra balancing, will help you augment the amount of energy your energy body can contain at any one time. You will get bigger and brighter as seen from our side.

Also, your work as a healer will benefit from the additional sensory, empathetic, and intuitive awareness such expansion brings. Your bright inner light is often enough to catalyze healing in another.

Being brilliant is more than being bright. Brilliance in your life and work is the fruit of spiritual awakening. Becoming brighter is a result of radiating the love wavelength.

Chakra Balancing Practice

Practice with me now. Take a deep breath through the nose and exhale through the mouth, making a sound with your voice. Repeat until you feel yourself drop into or contact the hum of the energy body. Take your time scanning the levels of your energy from head to toe and back again.

Now find the energy center that is vibrating the least and the one that is vibrating the most. Breathe into the center that is vibrating the least and needs an increase in energy. See it begin to fill with light and spin a bit faster, increasing its vibration.

Next, put your attention on the center vibrating the most. Send some of that energy up or down to the slower center. If there are other centers between these two, breathe into each one to raise its vibration as well.

Cycle your attention and breath from one center to another until they are closer in vibration levels. You may want to put your hands on or slightly above the two centers, one on the higher and the other on the lower center. Feel the changes as you bring them more closely into balance.

Now focus on the slower center, and ask your Higher Self, "Why is this center vibrating more slowly?" Simply ask and breathe into the center repeatedly until you receive a response. It may come to you as a thought, a feeling, a word, a sentence, or a picture in your mind's eye. Express that realization, out loud or inwardly, and allow full understanding of that message to permeate your being. Ask for more guidance, if needed, to clarify your understanding.

Ask for guidance on how to heal whatever has caused the energetic congestion in that center and what you need to get the energy flowing there again. You can ask your Higher Self, "What must I change to bring full energy to this area?" Note the answers as they come, continuing to breathe into the area. When you feel a sense of relief, give thanks for the insights received.

Use your imagination and these insights to heal that energy center. Imagine what the healing looks like, feels like, or sounds like. Notice how this changes the center's energy level. In your mind's eye, play out various scenes in which you are implementing the advice you received from Spirit to increase the energy in this center. As you mentally rehearse, notice which of the practices you are exploring works best for you. How does it feel now?

You may remember a time when you felt strongly empowered in this center. If you do, return to that time again. Feel the empowerment now that you experienced during that earlier experience. Hold it in your center, and sense the changes there. Imagine the center full of light, surging like a stream through your core to that center. Bask in that light. Appreciate its divine flow.

Now, in your mind's eye, examine the energy field around that center. Use your intention and attention to seal any leaks in that energy field. Go slowly, lovingly, using your attention to recognize leaks and mend them. You may want to use sound, words, and/or touch to heal them. Ask for guidance if needed.

Memories of what caused the leaks may surface as you are healing them. Recognize, acknowledge, and honor the memories, then send them out of your system and back to Source. Feel them if you must, but then clear them by letting them go, allowing them to be whisked out of your field as you heal your center and enter a higher vibration.

What will remind you to practice this new way of shifting and amplifying your energy in this energy center? Does it help to give this new insight or practice a name?

Choose that name right now. Continue in this moment to practice this process in order to anchor your new approach to healing this center and reinforce the fresh awareness it has brought you.

Now return to your new, higher conscious state and stand on your feet, integrating your increased energies for the rest of your day.

Thank you for this practice, Aion.

You are welcome. Practice this with yourself and others. This will accelerate your ability to visit us on our side of the veil. In no time at all, you will be holding much larger amplitudes of energy for your spiritual pleasure.

Healing through the imagination is quite a trick.

The trick is no trick. Your imagination is more powerful than your rational mind. Imagining a state of being brings you there. Visualizing makes it so on some level of your reality. If you can modulate your frequency to match what you visualize, you can enter that reality. Then the question is, can you hold that frequency and the energy level required, bringing that which you imagine into your life?

This is why chakra balancing is so transformational. A coherent, integrated, and fully charged energy field allows for the highest levels of manifestation. This explains why we in Spirit want for nothing. To manifest anything, we simply imagine it. Can you imagine?

How do you spell relief? N – O – W. There is no substitute.

21

Speaking with One Voice

"You are the captain, the navigator, and the mate on your ship of soul, and you can sail wherever you wish in the ocean of consciousness."

~ Aion

Aion, I'm feeling a bit under the weather, underpowered. I feel I am losing momentum.

You have slowed a bit in your practice, but think of your momentum as an endless arc of growth. You are fine and doing well enough. So be well! Tap into your healing power and cure yourself. You know how.

With this, Aion began to sing. It was a song I knew well from my time in a university acapella singing group, all about the need to believe in love from above. I felt myself humming along with Aion to the oldie, my spirits lifting a little.

Thank you, Aion. I had forgotten that song from my college days.

Not really. You can't forget anything. It is all recorded in your soul. Think of memories as strings of radiant pearls wrapping around and around the spark of Source, your soul. Each of these pearls stores a memory by retaining a frequency link to the related wave of consciousness from that experience. Every single moment you have experienced exists on these winding, interwoven strands of memory, all the way back to the moment your soul came forth from Source.

This is an imprecise description but, in any event, each soul can tune in to any strand of consciousness. This provides a library of recordings for reliving or re-experiencing any event, down to the quantum level.

Nothing is lost. All realizations, opportunities for learning, and perceptions are available, all the time. And nothing is truly forgotten. This is why you can feel comfortable letting go of the past. Your soul retains the learning you gained from your experience. That knowledge is always available to you for spiritual advancement when you learn to access it.

Is this the Akashic Record, where all knowledge and learning are stored?

Yes and no. The idea that all thoughts and events are recorded is correct, but they are not in a record book, presided over by a man with a white beard on the astral plane. Each soul is the "book" for its own experience, perceptions, and choices, and each soul is a unique, vital storehouse of wisdom and knowledge. Because all souls are collectively the One, all these recordings are available to every being. It sure beats the internet!

The implications are important. There is no divine being keeping tabs on whether you've been bad or good. The only judgment is self-judgment. Here comes the judge and the judge is you.

When a soul disincarnates, that soul carries out the entire soul review process in all its aspects. All facets of the diamond of self appear during this process to reflect the soul's development. Each facet of self brings a specific frequency of illumination to the process. You could think of this as a vast prism spreading a beam of celestial light out into all bands of the energy spectrum, visible and invisible, to clearly see the components of the whole, without disturbing the integrity of that whole.

What are these aspects, these facets of the self? I thought I was one, fully integrated soul.

Ah, another paradox. Just as each soul is both unique and inseparable from the One, so does each soul have multiple aspects which are inseparable from that soul. You contain fractals within fractals, aspects within aspects, waves within particles, and simultaneously, particles within those waves—on and on, and so on, ad infinitum. This is why taking your consciousness inward brings you outward and vice versa.

With this, Aion began singing the old Beatles riff about the inside being outside and the outside being in. Aion certainly was in a musical mood.

The aspects of which we sing are your multiple selves. I am one aspect of you, as are other beings you have encountered in your conscious and unconscious excursions. Your guides and angels also serve as aspects of you. Those souls on the path whose "books" you have "read," meaning the ones with whom you have merged by modulating your frequency in your sleeping and waking dreams, are now aspects of you, too. You realized Oneness with them, and they with you. Do you remember?

I did remember. Years before, I had been out of the body and encountering beings who looked like hooded Franciscan monks. Deep in meditation, these beings recited something as they walked down a green, grassy valley on a meandering, white pebble path. I found myself walking up that path, toward them, wearing a brown robe tied with a rough rope sash. I stared down at the simple rope sandals on my feet as I walked, fervently reciting my own recollections and stories from my lives.

As I approached one monk, we locked eyes, and my heart opened to this sincere being. As we stood face to face, I felt a deep respect for him. With a slow nod of his head, I felt him beam that same respect back to me. We each took a step forward, and suddenly we were occupying the same space.

All his stories flowed into me as if I was living them. And I could sense all my memories flowing into him. We each took another step forward and were separate again, me now further up the hill, him now down below me.

We turned, facing each other, our eyes literally glowing with gratitude, deep respect, and acceptance, each for the other, who was no longer an "other." We were One, each carrying both sets of stories, memories, and realizations. And it went even deeper. I understood that his story and mine, now our story, also contained the stories of countless others with whom we had previously shared our memories.

I cannot describe the impact of that merging.

Aion, at first I thought of each of us as a book of knowledge. With time, I have come to realize we are all encyclopedias, even entire libraries, vast collections of the soul's experiences.

The realm you were in during this experience is a place of knowledge, deep memories, and conscious reflection. Those beings you encountered serve as repositories of all wisdom. They help spread the Word by expanding the consciousness of each being who requests a melding of the souls. This is their purpose.

The one with whom you merged is now an aspect of you which helps you achieve your purpose. He is available to support you on your path, as you are available for him on his.

I feel I am a living book, just like those monks reciting their stories on that white, pebbled path.

Yes, indeed you are a book. And you are Self-published. You and all beings have the ability to tap into any of your soul's aspects to accelerate growth.

Are all these aspects actually conscious parts of us?

Consciousness takes many forms. Not all forms of consciousness are what you would consider a being.

Does it matter to you if the voice in your head is from me or if it rises from your subconscious mind? If you are giving that voice airtime in your head, then it will likely impact you, regardless of its origin. That is because the impact comes from you, not from outside of you. You create your reality.

Humans spend a lot of time analyzing their universe, parsing it into levels and hierarchies like species, genus, and phylum, to gain a sense of control and understanding. They cannot see life as it really exists. Actually, all human souls are on a level playing field, with all of the resources and support anyone could ever need to return to Source.

Hierarchy does not exist. That is a concept created by the human mind. All is sacred, all is divine. When we speak of spirit beings, angels, archangels, Over-soul, and the Godhead, we are using human terms to describe a divine reality that knows none of these distinctions. It is all God-energy, and we are One. Yes, we have individual souls, but we are not identified with those souls. We have personal roles, but we all share the same mission: To return all consciousness back to Source.

So to address your question, all aspects of your soul are as real as you make them, for they are all you. You can utilize these aspects to clarify motivation, learn soul lessons, and accelerate spiritual growth. The key is to speak with One Voice. This means aligning all the aspects of yourself, all of its energies and consciousness, into one single point of light that is your Being.

Integrating Soul Aspects

You might consider doing an inventory of all your soul's aspects. Then give each one a voice. Allow them to express their opinions and their wisdom. Most often, they are not all in agreement or aligned on your soul's purpose. This simply means you still have inner soul work to do.

Some aspects of yourself you have long ignored. Other aspects are less developed compared to the ones which you may have relied upon more frequently in day-to-day life. You may find some repressed aspects of the soul feeling hurt, resentful, or angry.

Most often, you can bring these aspects of yourself up to speed and reintegrate them with the new frequency you are entering. Sometimes, however, you will need to return some aspect to Source, a release that restores it to its original perfection. This is an act of completion and compassion, though you may need to grieve the loss of "that which was me" for a time. You will also need to align to the new frequency any aspects of yourself that relied on the old habit for comfort or sustenance.

You may also discover aspects that have come from loved ones, friends, or teachers to whom you have been particularly attached. These adopted aspects have an impact on your consciousness as well. Consider cutting the cord that binds them to the soul, allowing some of these aspects to return to Source.

Again, these aspects are impressions and fragments left over from lifetimes of experience and contact with all kinds of beings. Clarifying and clearing your energy body will naturally resolve many of these aspects. You are learning to let go of that which is not vibrating in the soul's highest frequency. Retain only the facets that reflect the highest light. You can think of this as polishing the facets of your diamond self.

Remember, there is no judgment of good and bad here. It is simply a matter of fit, not fault. Ask yourself, "Is this aspect a fit for me now?" You can also think of aspects as ideas, archetypes, self-identifications, and beliefs that you have held at different stages of growth. As you reach a new level of frequency, these aspects may no longer define you and may now be holding you back from speaking with the power of One Voice.

Heal and seal the leaks that drain your attention. It is a simple choice. Ask yourself, "Does putting my attention on this add to or distract from my feeling of connection?" The multiverse always provides marvelous feedback. It's instantaneous, no waiting required! Learn to discern, "Is it this or that?"

The work is to shed these old skins and grow a new one. Peeling away the layers of self that cannot vibrate at your new, higher frequency allows you to reach new levels of energy. With acceptance, the new frequency becomes your new norm. This is a continuous process of expanding boundaries, one in which all beings must engage to return to Source.

When your energy reaches the finest levels of vibration, boundaries disappear. Before this, the membrane of your energy field is its personal veil. As that membrane expands, it becomes more porous, until it finally dissolves. Limitations disappear and consciousness expands, spreading throughout the multiverse and merging with Source.

If you think of that membrane or energy field as a container, then strive for it to be a continually expanding, leak-proof vessel. Human beings are indeed vessels for Spirit, but in ways that most do not understand.

For one, it is the energy body, in conjunction with the physical body, that serves as the true vessel for Spirit. And your energy body is not an empty vessel, like a jar to fill. Promoters of organized religions rely on this image because they want followers to see themselves as passive receivers, and the religion as the source of Spirit.

But souls are not empty. They are full of Spirit, which is available to all in any moment. As we have been discussing, all souls also hold memories of their growth, including the moment each one came forth from Source. They contain memories of contacts with an untold number of consciousness beings, which are, just like them, on the path back to Source. The memories that are most powerful and most influential upon a soul are the aspects about which we have been speaking.

We encourage you, then, to see your energy body not as an empty container, but rather, as your ship, the vessel in which you travel the high seas. In all cases, you pilot your own vessel. It is your unique soul, with its free will, that sets the course of your growth. You are the captain, the navigator, and the mate on your ship of soul, and you can sail wherever you wish in the ocean of consciousness.

Cast off and set sail toward the guiding star of Source!

22

Learning to Herd Birds

"Your students are your flock, and you are their herder. But they are not sheep. They are a glorious flock of winged souls."

~ Aion

Aion, *I want to thank you again for bringing this incredible information through me. I feel very honored and humbled.*

Stevie Ray, it is our hope to help you feel more comfortable in sharing our message by reminding you that this information is not up to you. Although it seems as though you have an innate knowing for much of it, that sense of an innate knowing comes from your connection to Spirit.

Your students are your flock, and you are their herder. But they are not sheep. They are a glorious flock of winged souls. It is your role to help them find their flight path as they migrate back to Source.

It is your task to be a herder of birds. Herding birds is an effort, but it is well worthwhile. You will find it quite fulfilling as well as occasionally frustrating. You are already good at this, and there is nothing for you to do in order to prepare.

Just how does one herd birds?

The best way to get birds to flock is with birdseed. We will provide the seeds of inspiration, and it is for you to scatter this nourishment for their well-being.

Aion, even with so much practice now, many times I still forget your teachings and get caught up in the past or the future. How can I possibly help people be present if I can't stay here myself?

It is not on you to be the perfect model. Who could? It is your job to point the way. To do that, you will need to be present, at least in passing.

What? In passing? Aion, do you mean dying?

No, by referring to being present in passing, I don't mean dying consciously—though that can be in the cards for you, if you wish. I mean entering the moment and reentering the moment as frequently as you can. This feels blissful for you and, even if intermittent, serves as a powerful guidance system, both for you and those you instruct.

Make no bones about it. Enlightenment is not an entertaining fad. Nor is it a pursuit for dabblers. A single moment of awakening enriches your consciousness, but it won't bridge the divide between worlds. Only by stepping off the cliff and walking on air, fully trusting the buoyant energy of Spirit for a lift, can you cross that chasm. It is the difference between a pole vault and a rocket lifting off. The pole-vaulter will return to Earth, but the rocket will gain enough momentum to reach escape velocity.

Escaping the gravity of the mind gives you the momentum to pass through the veil. The momentum of the moment is momentous!

How can a moment have momentum? Isn't a moment still and quiet?

Each moment is uniquely flavored. Nothing in creation is standing still. Vibration and movement are everywhere and every when.

It is your mind that is suddenly still and quiet in an aware moment. You visualize a moment as a bubble around you, shutting out the distractions of life, but really it is your consciousness expanding past the noise of the mind.

Latch on to the movement of Spirit energy, and its flow will pull you along, increasing your frequency until it resonates with the present moment. This flow of energy accelerates your consciousness, until life around you seems to slow and lose its pull. This is anti-gravitas, a lightness of being, being en-lighten-ed.

Resonating with the frequency of divine light brings the realization that the Now is the only thing that is. All the rest is a hallucination, a product of the ego-mind. Compared to the speed of the Now, the mind is slow. This is why increasing your frequency is so vital to liberating your soul.

A faster vibration reaches escape velocity from the pull of the personality. It launches the soul on a trajectory toward the Beings of Light and the Great Central Sun. This is what I mean by saying moments have momentum. Presence moves at the speed of Spirit. In the momentum of presence, time disappears, and space collapses. There is no time between here and there. Now that's acceleration!

You may not realize it, but you could write books of celestial wisdom in a single weekend if you become able to hold your full attention in a high frequency moment.

That would be a long moment.

There is only one moment, and it is the one you are experiencing. You are always perceiving and creating your reality. Whichever string of reality you are following, there are always other potentialities you could realize in that same moment.

So what will it be, football on TV or the direct experience of God?

Do I have to make a choice between them? I can't believe I'm saying this to you, Aion, but I am really into football this season. Do I have to give it up to advance spiritually?

We sense resistance coming on. Are you really more identified with your football team's progress than with the progress of your healing team?

Of course not. Why do you put it that way?

We put it that way because your clarity is dependent on the quality of your attention and intention. If you really want to heal and share our messages with others, the degree of focus, the frequency of your energy, and the amplitude of its flow must be high. This requires patience, perseverance, and practice. It is an investment in time and attention that will yield unlimited returns. You can't do that in the stock market!

Your current stamina for focusing is about 20 minutes. After that, your energy field begins to contract because your busy mind regroups and interrupts the flow of thought packets from us, reducing your receptivity. Think of it as static on a phone. A crystal clear line of communication requires a quiet mind and the utmost in openness.

It's not that you can't watch football and also download our messages. But you are asking for a rapid ramp-up in capabilities, and that means more practice than you have been giving it. Let's say about double the quality and quantity. This can happen throughout the day as well as in concentrated meditation.

Use the tools we have given you. Become an expert in moving your own energy at any time, in all situations. You are a change agent for Spirit and are called to aid us in helping other souls move along their path. This is a big part of your training.

Think of it as a workout for the soul, flexing and building the muscles of your attention. It won't develop your biceps, but it will develop your tri-modal organ of perception. As your focus and consciousness expand, we will be able to communicate with you for extended periods of time. At some point, with sincere development on your part, we could be in constant communication mode through you.

I would like that very much.

Are you sure, after more than six hours of football on TV? Mull it over and get back to me on that.

The only limit on our availability to you is your attention. We have all the time needed, or we would have all the time if time existed. It's the attention and holding the frequency we are coming in on that is the key. You have unlimited capability for attention and can easily expand from where you are with practice.

In terms of teaching, there is much to be done. Where you begin or which topics you explore matters less than just getting started. You have no reason to rush; simply move forward with focus. Find a pace at which you can stay present. Our goal is that as many students as possible should be given the opportunity to learn these concepts and skills.

You make the effort, and we will guide you. You only have to stay one breath ahead of your students. We will provide the healing energies to help the students experience for themselves the power of Spirit in action. Remember, the experience, not just the words, is important for them. Each will have his or her internal healing during the course of the training. This is a gift beyond price, and students who are ready will recognize it as such.

This is not work but a sacred joy. Herding birds is your purpose and the reason you have returned to the physical form. You will have the time of your life as you join your flock and soar with them to new heights in Spirit.

23

The Transformed Human

"Transformed humans look a lot like anyone else.
It's just that they glow."

~ Aion

One night, I dreamed of electric-white hands holding out a beautiful bowl of beaten gold. In the bowl, a mound of orbs, each just a little smaller than a golf ball, glowed in swirling colors. When I saw them, I thought of the aggie shooter marbles I played with as a kid. But I knew without asking that these were not childhood toys.

In that vivid, more-than-dream state, a voice spoke. "Choose one," that voice directed, filling me with energy and light. I knew at once it was Aion speaking.

Thank you for visiting me this morning in my dream, Aion. I feel so healed, so full and grateful, so peaceful. In the dream, I understood that I could begin a new life by picking one of the small glowing globes from the bowl you were holding. After choosing one, I felt transformed. What was going on?

Those radiant globes are pearls of wisdom. They contain deep experiential knowledge that surpasses any understanding and communicates directly into the soul.

You have chosen well, and you are transformed.

I felt the energy in it go into the area between my second and third chakras, the Star of Life. A deep tranquility is developing there, a relaxed, calm, and connected feeling that makes me smile.

You are being healed from the inside out. This pearl of great price is a gift to you from Source. Keep it with you always.

Once again, Aion was using the words of my guide, Laughter, on my journey through other realms so many years before. The memory of that experience echoed through me now.

I will, and I am so grateful. What is it?

This is for you to discover and uncover. This is for you to know. It is a healing for you and a healing to share with the world. No need to fret about it, though. You are assimilating it as we speak.

It is, of course, an answer to your request to know your purpose. And by "know," I mean, to realize, to actualize, to manifest your purpose. This will change your life dramatically, but you already know that is happening.

The globes in the bowl were luminous, transparent. They radiated a glowing warmth. When I put my hand above each one, I received a felt sense of what it contained.

Three stood out to me, radiating more brightly than the others. The one I was most attracted to rose up to meet my hand, then sent energy flowing through my body, entering through the area around my navel and filling my belly with light. No wonder I felt so full, so radiantly happy!

The one I picked seemed like a natural choice. Why? And what about the other two?

You chose as you must, from the consciousness that you are. The fit is perfect.

The other two are available for you, too, when you are ready. No need for buyer's remorse since all knowledge is available to every soul. You lack for nothing, and you left nothing behind.

Really? There are two more for me?

I kid you not; there is always more from Source.

You are big enough for all of them. The only question is when, and the answer is always in the Now in which you find yourself.

How's that for enigmatic? Are you finding your Self yet?

I am.

Well answered! Find your Higher Self, realize the I Am, and you will have all questions answered. You have every opportunity to transform, if you so desire. All beings have this opportunity. Every strand of possibility is open to each soul in every moment.

You're opening is coming in stages to keep from overwhelming your nervous system. Each new round of clearing raises your frequency. There is no replacement for moving congested energy and increasing the volume and flow of energy through the energy body.

Yes, many other types of work are important for self-development, including psychology, psychotherapy, bodywork, and all kinds of healing for the physical body, especially its nerves and cells. There truly is better living through chemistry! That is to say, metabolism, brain chemistry, and the electrochemical processes of the body are critically important for maximizing spiritual energy. It is much easier to move your energy when the physical body is healthy than when it is sick.

But most people live day-to-day in subpar health. This, combined with a lack of attention on what they are feeling in the moment, restricts the amount and frequency of the energy flowing through them.

Fortunately, you have many ways to remedy the situation. Maintaining cellular health is your responsibility to your own bliss.

We're not saying progress is impossible when you are ill. Quite the contrary. Many make significant spiritual progress during illness. It just seems more difficult from the perception of the person who is ill because the energy centers of the body metabolize spiritual energy and, though independent of the physical body, also link to it.

This is why aligning and healing the energy centers creates healing in the physical body. It is also why physical ailments affect your energetic processes. Though you have the physical body and the interpenetrating subtle energy body, the effect is of one united organism housing the spark of Source.

All of your energy bodies play their part and make their choices based on the consciousness of the being. Perhaps it seems strange to hear that these linked bodies can make their own choices, but this is, in effect, what happens. These choices occur on many levels of consciousness across multiple timelines.

Thus, an immediate cause for disease, disfigurement, or challenge to any one of a person's bodies may not be obvious. Somewhere, some when, an aspect of that being decided to accept a challenge for the soul's development. It is impossible for another to judge or understand these decisions, so don't try.

Simply allow the energy to move through the body, aligning and clearing its centers, and everything else will follow. This doesn't need to be too fancy. Theories are useful for providing comfort when approaching the unknown, but it is direct experience of energy from Source that transforms.

What does a transformed human look like?

Transformed humans look a lot like anyone else. It's just that they glow. The pure light of Spirit radiates through them. This glow communicates. It spreads, igniting an inner spark in all souls that it touches. It is the light of en-light-enment, elevating all consciousness.

In your world, you normally think of your major achievements, your good deeds, or even the spiritual practices you perform as your purpose. But we say, this flame, this radiating bliss is the true purpose of all beings. Each moment of bliss, every experience of true, inner, divine love raises the consciousness of all. Can you imagine a purpose greater than this?

At work, getting a raise is a proud moment, a well-earned recognition for achieving the goals of the business. In spiritual development, your job is to be in the moment. The raise is a raise in frequency. The reward is increased energy, aliveness, and joy. And this reward reaches to the entire extended family of souls throughout the multiverse. Your job is to return to Source, and you advance in every moment.

Pause for a moment and be aware of your surroundings, your feelings, and your energy. That's all it takes to do your job. Feel the energy flowing through you. Breathe into it deeply. Find any spot that draws your attention and breathe into it. Release it. Ask for more energy, and it appears.

Make it your own.

This energy is your friend, your raft in the gentle stream of consciousness. Float along with this current of Now. Allow it to gently move you. It is so relaxing, yet so energizing. Bring your attention to the top of your head and connect to the infinite stream flowing down from above. Relax and float in the warmth of connection, head to toe and back up again.

Be with it.

Breathe. Simply be.

Thank you. You are now achieving your purpose. We here in Spirit are so grateful for all who make this energetic connection. You radiate like a beacon of light across time and space, healing and uplifting all that is throughout the multiverse. Living on purpose is staying in the moment, fully connected to this bliss. Not a bad job, is it?

Definitely not. Aion, you're the best recruiter in the business.

No recruiting necessary. The job has always been yours.

24

My Future's Future Self

"All future threads exist in the present, even your future's future self."

~ Aion

Aion, you have frequently mentioned that enlightenment is available in an instant. Doing all these practices each day seems linear, a plodding approach. Please help me understand the seeming discrepancy here.

It is time for the paradox of time again.

You are where you are on your path back to Source. The many layers of remembrances and impressions that are what you think of as "you" hold your awareness in that place, that frequency. Often, your consciousness is out of the present, and so you are subject to your own reality in time and space. This is your reality, not ours.

If you could release your reality all at once and move into the highest frequencies and the widest flow of etheric energy through your system, realizing your Higher Self would be instantaneous. Are you ready for that?

Yes and no. I want to do it, but I'm frightened. What will become of me if I go there?

Nothing and everything. Change and no change. Realization and imagination become one. There is no longer an illusion of separation, yet you retain a sense of Self. It is nothing because it is already so. It is everything because nothing remains of the limited you. It is change because you are now always in the unchanging moment. And all this is no change at all. You are in all ways present and in service to the One.

When you know, it is so.

One technique to experiment with is to increase the energy in the center of your forehead, your third eye. Bring the energy up to the forehead and then project it out ahead of yourself through your third eye. Allow that energy in front of you to open the most delightful, joyous, and highly energized path before you, so that with each step, you are walking on a path already created by you. It is as if you have your own entourage, an advance team clearing the way for your delight.

Learning to project your energy body has many benefits. One of the most important is that it provides you with a larger container for spiritual energy. This allows you to maintain a larger amplitude of energy, a greater flow with which you can advance your progress.

It is also important to remain aware of your connection to Earth and stay grounded while enjoying the experience of an expanded energy body. Remember, you are a bridge, and a bridge needs two anchors, one on either end of the span it crosses.

Aion, I think I need some help with the particulars. How does this bridge pass through the veil? And who crosses it coming from Spirit to Earth?

One way to look at the veil is to think of it as your fear. The veil is the interface, a transducer between your reality and ours. Coming from your side, energy must be stepped up in frequency, and from our side it must be stepped down for you to receive it in a way that makes sense in your reality.

However, if you had no fear, you would have no veil. Having no fear, you would not limit your energy. You could travel freely through dimensions and frequencies, enjoying the best of both worlds. The less fear you generate, the more love, the more energy you can contain. And it is this love that allows your field to grow big and wide.

The bridge you are building is an arc, a span of light that is your consciousness, anchored by your Over-soul on our side and by your soul's energetic field on yours. How wide that bridge is depends on how expansive an energy body you can sustain, which, in turn, depends on how grounded you can be. The wider the bridge, the easier it is for you and others to cross.

Breathe in. That's right, expand your energy now. Allow any momentary concerns or fears to simply flutter past and return back to Source. As your energy expands, so does your ability to see. You are seeing now, seeing much more of what you are creating, just a bit in front of yourself. Step into that creation, that new version of you.

Now I'm seeing the back of my head. I'm sitting at the front of a room, with a group of people seated around me. We are practicing together. You are speaking through me, educating us in the ways of Spirit. I'm explaining what I have learned about expanding the light body.

It is important for you to share your process with those who wish to ride the light. The bridge you are building is wide enough and strong enough to carry many souls to the experience of the other side. Then they can build their own bridges and carry many other souls across. There is no end to the amount of joy that can come of this, if you only step into that expanded future version of you.

Can you say more about seeing? I get the sense that the images I'm seeing right now are my own future.

Yes, they are futures you are creating, even as we speak.

Are they probable futures?

They exist for you as more than probabilities. By expanding the volume of your energy field, you can encompass many futures and step into any of them. The key is containing energy and channeling enough of its flow to unify and expand your field.

It is not about inflating your ego. Instead, grow the core energy of the Higher Self expressed through you, integrate all of your energy centers, and unify your energy bodies into a single, pulsating energy field. This is the direct experience of Spirit in the body. It provides enough creative power not just to see the future but to experience your future while also remaining in the Now. This is simultaneity. Welcome to our reality.

I'm not sure I'm getting all this. Is it correct to say...

I suggest you return to feeling it and frame your question from that state.

Ah, you see and are seeing—suddenly no question. In that state there is no question because you are the embodiment of the answer.

There is no need to try to create, no need to push the future. It emerges naturally out of the conscious expression of energy in the moment. All consciousness is an expression of Source. Every expression of consciousness is a reality that can be entered by the soul vibrating at a matching frequency. Then you see.

You have the capability of being an eyes-open, walking-around, living example of Spirit fully embodied. Many souls have this ability, but few would choose to exemplify it. Your choice to pursue this path is bringing you many benefits and exciting challenges. You have the opportunity to clear the slate, so to speak, and write a new history of you. This is you writing the history of your future in the Now.

OK, Aion, this is getting a little dense. Or perhaps I'm a little dense.

Allow me to explain. You writing the history of your future in the Now implies the "you" that is ahead even of the "future you," whom you are currently creating, can look back and instruct you in the present.

All future threads exist in the present, even your future's future self. Its understandings, skills, and abilities can be brought into the present. This is what we mean when we say there's no need to wait around and prepare. Multiple iterations of you have been doing this for eons already. You can tap into that wisdom right now if you can expand your mind, perceptions, and beliefs to accept this.

Let's take a little journey, a very short journey that will take no time at all, into your future, to connect with your future's future self. What does that version of you look like?

In my mind's eye, I watched a 15-foot sphere of golden light, full of motion and energy, approach. Delight washed over me as the sphere touched my energy field, hovering just a little above and in front of me. It radiated pure joy. I felt myself merge with it, and as I did, I knew intuitively that this indeed was my future's future self, capable of things I had never dared to dream I would be able to do—not in any lifetime, much less this one.

My future's future self has the ability to be in the body and also live as a timeless, space-less being. He or she, this genderless being, lives in Spirit and can enter into anyone's body, when asked, in order to create a shift for that individual. What's interesting about this is that we have jumped over the future me, which is closer to my present being.

Let's stay with the future's future you for now. What does this beautiful being have to say to you?

To say that this being began to speak would be misleading. Rather, a beautiful feeling tone filled our shared, resonant field as words welled up in my awareness in a effortless flow.

"Stevie Ray, my boy, you stand on the precipice of transformation. Take the leap and fly. You know in your heart of hearts that your angelic wings will support you, and you will rise like a condor with its vast wingspan.

"You have earned your wings. Feel free to leave the nest of your current identity and soar above any limitations you have held until now.

"I know you think your experiences have been majestic, but I am here to say these were only test flights. Your maiden voyage awaits you as you stand at the precipice. On one hand, you fear falling off the edge of your reality with no ground below. On the other, you face the chance to soar into limitless galaxies above, reaching heights you've never imagined.

"I see you have already made the choice. Release yourself now into the arms of Spirit. Become the energy that flows through you, and allow yourself to be carried on those angel wings.

"We in Spirit support you; we have always supported you and will always support you, for we are you. You have been preparing and are prepared for this journey. And without leaving the comfort of your chair, you can fly on wings of Spirit anywhere in the multiverse.

"This is as it should be and as it is.

"Call on me anytime, for I have lived your transformation and can guide you. You are really going to love this. It is a journey with no end and no beginning, a journey that goes nowhere and no when. This journey happens in the perpetual moment. It takes you away and leaves you where you are simultaneously.

"Allow me to enter your consciousness and provide you with the cellular memories of our transformation. May they be a resource encouraging you to take the leap and soar on wings of light."

With this, the golden sphere that had enveloped me slowly dissipated. Still reverberating, I slowly returned my attention back to my earlier conversation with Aion.

Oh, my God, I had no idea!

Yes, and you are not just getting the idea, you are the Idea. You are the "you to be," and you are the One You. As I am you, you, too, are the beloved One and Only You.

I'd say this is complicated, but I see now that it is not. It's just more than I expected. I want to ask, "Can I trust that future me?" But I already know the answer. There is no escaping the truth of my reality, regardless of the timeline in which it resides.

You have free will. You can make other choices, but they all lead back to the same Place in No Time and No Space.

Feel free to fly, as you will. Stay in this moment of divine love and appreciation. There is nothing greater.

I'm asking myself, "How do I take this all in? How do I integrate and ground this experience in my life?"

Live it! Love it! Accept yourself, because you can't leave your Higher Self. You are God enough, as you can see.

Yes, I am.

Well said!

Can you tell me about the self in between me in the present and my future's future self?

In good psychotherapist style, I will ask you, what do you know about that?

I thought you might.

I know I am bigger in the experience of Spirit. I can contain planets but not yet galaxies. My contact with Earth is less dense today than yesterday. I feel as though I don't have a permanent residence in a body.

This feels like a period of intense learning and growing. I am testing the limits of my abilities and encountering none. I expect to hit boundaries to cross, like the veil, but I can't find any. I pursue multiple probabilities, which become the realities in which I live. Everything seems possible. I experience no fear, which amazes me.

Everything is possible. Creativity has no limits. The limits you experience are those you put on your own imagination.

I feel my belief system is breaking down. It is liberating, like I'm free-falling from the sky. But the reality of the earth never rises up to meet me. I just keep falling through the atmosphere.

You have been there and done that. Though there was no T-shirt, you did come away with something. What is that?

It is the knowing deep inside that I need not fear falling down, for I am completely supported, held in the arms of Spirit.

I am falling up, waking up; I am falling in love, falling into love.

Yes, you are, and we welcome you with open arms.

Truly I did feel welcomed, overflowing with the joie de vivre of knowing myself in a way I never had before—from the future, looking back.

25

Releasing Resistance

"You do get what you wish for, so wish for the
highest frequencies, the greatest love,
and the brightest light."

~ Aion

The experience of my future's future self touched me in a way that
defies description. It went beyond words, into an experience of
cellular memories, not from a traumatic past but an expanded, un-
dreamed realm of possibility. My future's future self seemed vastly
ahead of the current "me," yet I could be inside of that self and express
it Now.

The encounter scrambled my brain—as it turns out, a very good
thing.

*I'm thinking about our conversation yesterday, and it seems to be getting very
esoteric and grandiose. I feel a little nervous about this. Could my ego be taking me
off track? Am I having delusions of grandeur?*

I thought we had addressed this earlier, but let's look at it again
more closely.

Your underlying concern is that all this talk about your future's
future self in Spirit is a loose thread in the fabric of your sanity. Pull
on it, and this whole conversation will unravel, with you finally seeing how deluded you have been to think you could be God, or even
God-like in Spirit.

Is that right?

Not to put too fine a point on it....

At the bottom of it, you still feel you are not worthy, not up to the task. But there is no task, no "oughta, coulda, woulda, shoulda." There is no requirement. There is only being, with nothing to do about it.

Simply be who you truly are in the moment. This is where you find your joy and the exquisite awareness of yourself as Spirit. This is enlightenment, where you lighten your load. So put down your backpack, release the weight of doing you have carried so diligently, and then you can fly.

You're saying I feel uncomfortable with my divine nature as a result of "not good enough" conditioning?

You were fed a line, and you took the bait. You bought into the straight and narrow, hook, line, and sinker. You accepted all that undue criticism, obeyed all those false rules, and took threats of damnation seriously, choosing to be a good little boy striving for a golden future.

But that version of the future you, the one you embodied even when you knew better, crushed your soul like a tin can. In all those years of fear of failure, the pain of loss, and suffering from lack of satisfaction, you kept yourself deluded, separate from the experience of God for which your soul so longed.

Now that seems crazy, doesn't it? But trying to be the Golden Boy did pay off in one way. Living in that excruciating pain helped you realize the value of your soul's freedom to choose. Now you know.

I do.

In your knowing, would you choose to go back and relive that all over again? Of course not. But what if, in your current state of realization, you risk repeating that same process of limitation on another level? All the same caveats, the same rational "gotchas," all the same false wisdom is still out there, waiting to bring your vision of the future you down to earth.

"Don't fly too high, Icarus, your wings will melt," they will say, as they always have. "Be careful what you wish for, you might get it," they will say.

These are not the voices of reason; they are the voices of reasons for why not to be your expansive Higher Self. Listening to these voices is what crushed your soul in the first place. Now that you have reclaimed it, fly high! Take to the sky and beyond.

You do get what you wish for, so wish for the highest frequencies, the greatest love, and the brightest light. Thou art God. God gets what God creates, no kidding. This is your divine nature.

God wants you to experience that you are All of That. This experience doesn't come from withholding the full grandeur of God from yourself. It comes from you being the grandeur, which is the birthright of the soul, the very reason you came forth from Source. But don't just take my word for it. Enter into that grandeur and see for yourself, just for the bliss of it.

This doesn't mean you have to sit in meditation all day. Quite the contrary. You can connect with Source at the grocery store just as well as in meditation if you are in the timeless moment. Where you put your attention determines your experience. Can you choose bananas and still experience your divine energy? Certainly!

Wherever you go, your energy body goes with you. Put your attention here, on the flow within you. Breathe into it as you smell that lovely loaf of rosemary sourdough bread. You may have a clair-olfactory experience! Let your senses carry your attention back to Spirit.

It is simply a choice. The choice is not between right and wrong, only between, "This is what I want to be feeling," and, "This is what I don't want to be feeling." If you want to feel Spirit, then identify with Spirit. Choose that which leads your attention back to Spirit energy within.

Releasing Resistance in Soul Aspects

Contact whatever sensation of resistance you may find within and breathe into it. Caress that area with your breath. Expand the energy there and sense the "what" of it. As you continue breathing into it, recognition of what it is will make itself known to you.

Name this aspect of yourself if you wish. Be curious. What is that aspect communicating to you? How is it feeling? What is it showing you?

Breathe some more. Now let this aspect of you know that you appreciate it.

Does the aspect you are working with want to move into this future with you, or would it rather be released into the loving arms of Source? If it wishes to return to Source, wish it well and let it go; spin it out of your body like a wisp of fog.

If you want to continue to include that aspect of you in your way of being as a resource for yourself, then get the aspect aligned to your Higher Self. Show the aspect your vision of a higher frequency version of you, the future's future you that lives along the new string of possibility you are creating.

Breathe into the new you. Allow your energy to redistribute itself, to vibrate and heal that leak in your field. Be with this new energy as it lifts, expands, and embraces you from the inside moving out.

Feeling better?

Oh, yes!

We are glad to see you delight in your energy, Stevie Ray. We care about you and are assisting in your soul integration, as you have requested. By immersing yourself in the energy, you will be able to integrate and bridge the gap between both worlds.

Never underestimate your ability. By now you understand. With our help, you can achieve everything you can dream. You can realize Spirit in the body. This changes your perception and opens many doors through which you can step into new realities.

Thank you, Aion. What other advice do you have for me?

Immerse yourself in the new energy you are experiencing. Balance practice with rest and relaxation. Find new and innovative ways to enter into the moment, where you will find your highest expression of joy and love in this lifetime.

For instance, by expanding your energy body around your physical body, you will find you are more aware of the guiding spirits around you and the energy available for your support. This will allow you to include your nearby spirit guides in your field. They are on your support team. This is very comforting and also raises your frequency.

Expand your field by breathing into it, seeing it glow with a golden energy, and feeling it as a corona around your physical body, expanding out several inches, then growing to several feet.

Of course, the field can get much larger than this as you strengthen your ability to contain larger amplitudes of energy. Bring Spirit energy in and radiate it out in a circulating current that integrates all of your energy bodies.

You are creating your own hot spring, a pool of relaxing, healing energy. We thank you for your willingness to put our simple advice to good use.

26

The Blue Pearl

"If you feel you are coming unglued, it's because those
aspects of you which are inappropriately stuck
to your soul are coming loose."

~ Aion

W hen we decided to put the house on the market, my wife had begun to notice luminous spheres appearing in photographs we
took around the property, what she called orbs. We went back through
all our old photos and saw that many of them had these same orbs in
them. We had never noticed.

In all honesty, I was a skeptic. Most science-minded folks insist
that orbs are a relic of the camera itself, evidence of nothing more than
the inner workings of the little point-and-shoot digitals that capture
the near-infrared range of light. But my wife's enthusiasm for them
led me to explore the phenomenon with her, and the movie about orbs
that I watched with her sparked us to begin experimenting.

As a lark, we would go into the back yard to "play with the orbs." I
was doing this with her as a way to help the two of us connect through
the growing strain in our relationship. I more or less thought the
whole thing was a fantasy. But over time, I realized that the more we
called the orbs, the more they showed up in our photographs. In one
photograph I took, my wife actually disappeared behind a whole cloud
of orbs. Could they actually be beings with consciousness that we were
interacting with and drawing to ourselves?

Even though we saw the orbs increase as we put our attention on
them, I would not say my experience made me a believer. But it did

open a door for me. I began to consider the possibility that the phenomenon could be something more than just a trick of the camera.

Even so, nothing I saw in our backyard could have prepared me for my face-to-face encounter with an orb.

My wife and I were reading in bed. I wasn't sleepy and got up to go to the bathroom. Afterwards, I paused briefly in the living room, still not ready to go back to bed. With my hands resting on the back of our leather club chair, I stared softly into the darkness. Suddenly a small, glowing sphere, about the size of a golf ball and cobalt blue, appeared across the room.

The sphere hovered near the ceiling, then signaled me by flashing and changing its form into a disc about a foot in diameter. Inside the disc, mandala-like patterns appeared in undulating, concentric rings, as though bubbling up from a churning molten core. I thought of light shining through the body of a jellyfish, revealing translucent organs in constant, rippling motion. Simply put, it seemed alive.

The disc quickly collapsed in on itself, becoming once again a glowing sphere that slowly approached me. Traveling an irregular route, it took five or six seconds to cross the 12 feet to where I was standing.

Though the room was dark, the sphere was easy to follow with my eyes. Its bright, cobalt blue light glowed from inside, giving it a penumbra, almost like an aura. It hovered just below the ceiling.

"It's persisting," I thought, amazed. I was expecting it to flash and streak away.

I could feel some fear rising, but the energy streaming through me felt glorious. Every hair was standing on end, and goose bumps covered my entire body, despite the warmth of the night air. When it stopped directly over my head, I was looking straight up at it, suspended just a couple of feet above me.

I could see it clearly. The inside of the sphere seemed to have waves of deep blue colors moving within it. Then it flashed again into the orb shape, about 4 inches across, with a beautiful, complicated pattern of symmetrical lines at its center.

It radiated energy down on me, bathing me in a beautiful and powerful glow. I stared at it, breathing slowly and intentionally, simply taking it in. I realized that it intended for the energy it was beaming down to go into my crown chakra, so I looked down, receiving a big jolt through my system. When I looked back up, I expected it to be gone. But it was still there! It coalesced back into the glowing sphere and slowly wandered about 6 feet away from me, then simply disappeared.

The whole thing took about 12 seconds. I was stunned. Still vibrating, I went back to the bedroom and told my wife what I had just seen. The next day, I began a conversation with Aion about the experience.

So did I actually see what I thought I did last night, standing in my living room?

You saw the Blue Pearl, The Rupa, with your own two eyes. How can you doubt that? It was a gift, an initiation into the next stage of your soul's unfolding.

I saw it. I experienced it. I received it. What does it mean?

What do you know about it?

I know it had consciousness and intent.

So is seeing believing?

This is hard for me to integrate. All these years of crying out to see and know Spirit. But actually seeing it with my own eyes, in my own living room, is still hard to accept. It's as though a big part of me has never really believed in the reality of Spirit. To recognize this about myself feels very disappointing.

On the other hand, I have to admit that a different part of me now feels like I belong with all the other crazies who tell outlandish stories of their otherworldly adventures.

Go ahead and say it.

You know, the people with their stories of encounters with UFOs, abductions, conversations with God, angels, and aliens. The whole over-the-top New Age lot. It feels good to get that off my chest. Thanks.

Now you have had your own encounter—not in a dream but fully awake and in 3-D. What do you make of that? Who are you now? What box will you put yourself in to preserve the last threads of your old identity?

Soon you will be fully able to see. Seeing is the convincer for most humans, though it is sight in a very limited range. Still, seeing can be believing.

You are unraveling a mystery. Each gift from Spirit propels you closer to seeing the truth, to believing in who you already are. If you feel you are coming unglued, it's because those aspects of you that are inappropriately stuck to your soul are coming loose. Now you can lose them. Release them back to Source. Keep only that which vibrates at your new frequency.

What do you know now?

I know this is real, and my life is changing radically. We have put our house on the market. Neither of us has earned any appreciable income in the last year, but I can't work on anything except this book, beginning to teach, and the healing work that calls to me. Starting a job would be so painful and feel so much like going backwards that it seems ridiculous.

Now, at almost 60 years old, I am finally pursuing my quest to know my True Self. I toyed with it before, but I allowed myself to be seduced by my ego—money, career, and a false sense of self.

Yes, the matrix had you. Now you are free. Be all of who you are. If that unbelieving part is no longer a fit for you, release it now.

That's right. Feels good, doesn't it? Judge not yourself or others and you will remain free.

So, besides all this spiritual stuff being real, the UFO stuff is real, too?

It is, but this is all a matter of understanding. Increasing your frequency naturally allows you to see more, to know more of what some aspect of you already knows. Did you really think Elijah ascended into the Heaven in a fiery chariot? That was a space ship.

Remember passing into Spirit. It's quite a load-off, a veritable liftoff. This is much like the energy you were experiencing last night. Vibrations coursing through your nervous system, waves of energetic tingles radiating outward from your core, a heightened sense of awareness and connection to Spirit energy. You can almost see Spirit on the other side.

27

Through My Walls

"The Ashtar Command watches over the awakened ones on
Earth so they will not be distracted from growing
into their roles in the divine plan."

~ Aion

My experience with the Blue Pearl had stretched me well beyond
my comfort zone. Before it happened, I thought of topics like
the Ashtar Command as make-believe for grown ups, the New Age
equivalent to jargon used by Trekkies or the Comic-Con crowd.

Now I wasn't so sure. After my visit from the Blue Pearl, I could no
longer deny the reality of dimensions beyond this one. Even though I
still didn't feel comfortable talking about things like aliens and space
ships, my experiences had opened me to understanding my own encounters in a new light.

*Someone asked me about the Ashtar Command. I'll admit, this kind of thing
is still pretty "out there" for me. But I do find that I am more curious about it after
my experience with the Blue Pearl. What can you tell me about the Ashtar Command?*

My brother Ashtar valiantly leads the Command. They are Soul
Guardians who oversee the shift in vibration underway on the planet. They, along with a host of others, are engineering the magnificent transition that is already underway. These souls have nothing
but your best interests in mind.

Why do they watch over us?

You are a part of the network of light workers needed to help see this earth plane transition through to a smooth completion. We need this force on Earth so that we may work through each of you, as you allow. We have much work to do with the souls on Earth to foster this transition.

Some are not in alignment with the galactic plan for Earth and her inhabitants. These misaligned energies also have free will and are pursuing their interests in and on the planet in a variety of dimensions. It is our job to maintain the balance throughout the multiverse so that consciousness can continue to evolve, experiencing itself in its self-knowing. The Ashtar Command watches over the awakened ones on Earth so they will not be distracted from growing into their roles in the plan for divine awakening.

Growing the circle of awakened souls is your role, your part to play. But it is not a play. It is the real thing, as real as it gets. There are many on the verge of seeing and knowing who can use the support of this brotherhood, this cadre of healers, teachers, and soul nurturers, if you will. Indeed, these light workers will also need rejuvenation, recreation, and support. The circle of light must grow.

Rest assured. You are well-protected and in no danger.

Would you explain more about the misaligned energies?

They are souls in crisis. For their own reasons, they have rejected returning to Source. God's love burns just as brightly for these souls as for all others. They have simply chosen more convoluted paths than most. Even though they outwardly refuse the light, they are still serving Source because they are still collecting experiences and growing in awareness. They also serve to highlight the contrast between light and dark. To appreciate limitless bliss, you must have experienced the pain of separation.

For what reasons would they reject the bliss of merging with Source?

There are many. Some have become so enamored with their various aspects that they deny the desire to ascend. Others punish themselves. Even though they love God, they feel deeply unworthy and think of themselves as pollution in the stream of consciousness that God could not purify. The beings stuck in a single focus of consciousness are another type, forever exploring inward, ignoring everything outside of themselves. In counterpoint, others do just the opposite, solely focusing outward. And many in this category want to expand their own power to the detriment of others' free will. We are here to keep all this in balance.

Safety is not a concern. As we said, you are protected. Continue to call on us. We are always here for you.

Also, you may recall, you have met some of the Ashtar Command already.

I thought those were dreams.

You were out of the body at night, having conscious excursions into a nearby dimension in which the Ashtar Command frequently resides.

I knew just what Aion was referencing. It had happened years before I first made contact with Aion. I had been in bed, ostensibly meditating but actually more just drifting in and out of sleep, when I found myself suddenly transported to another place.

Even though I seemed to be dreaming, I felt fully present and awake. I stood in a warm, arched corridor, about 12 feet across. Its walls were smooth and seamless from the floor, across the curve of its ceiling, and back down to the floor on the opposite side. Its featureless panels emanated a cool, even light.

Around me, a crowd of around 30 people had gathered, all of them wearing jumpsuits in vivid primary colors, and most of them unremarkable. Only two stood out, a man and a woman, both thin, tall, and blue-eyed, with pale skin and long blond hair. This radiant couple stepped through the group to the front. Both measured close to 7 feet in height, dressed all in white, wearing tight pants and stylish, high-collared tunics that brushed their thighs. They were the essence of cool.

As they introduced themselves—and I cannot remember their names—I could feel a sense of anticipation and excitement from the crowd behind me. The couple suggested we begin walking, with the people in jumpsuits following behind the three of us down the glowing corridor. We discussed physics and astrophysics, philosophy and consciousness as we walked, a conversation both stimulating and remarkable, despite its casual tone. The scene ahead of us, an endless hallway curving always just a little toward the left, never changed.

At some point, the two looked at me, then at each other, and I felt a sense of deflation. A low-pitched "Aaaw... " moved through the crowd behind us like air let out of a balloon. One of the two asked me, "Is there something you want to say or do to complete this visit?"

"No, no, this has been lovely," I replied sunnily.

They glanced at each other with a dismayed look, one that seemed to me to say, "Oh, well. It was worth a try."

Then I was fully awake, still sitting up in my bed.

The next night the same thing happened—meditation in bed, then the corridor and the tall, almost angelic couple. The crowd was smaller this time, maybe 20, but still charged with a feeling of expectation. Again we took a walk down the featureless, curving hallway. Again the air went out of the crowd as the couple stopped our conversation to ask if I wanted to say or do anything to complete my time with them. And again I felt their letdown as I politely declined saying or doing anything more, just before waking up in my bed.

When it happened the third night in a row, the crowd walking behind us had dwindled to seven or eight. By now, I knew I was not having some crazy abduction experience and felt more present and calm than I had on previous nights. As I sensed us nearing the end of our walk, I found myself compelled to speak.

"I feel like you are disappointed with me somehow."

They did not respond.

In the awkward silence that followed, I took a deep breath and looked at the space around us. "What I'm noticing," I continued, "is that there are no doors and no windows. Only this glowing hallway."

Just then, I thought of the transformation conference, and the pulsing field of light in front of me that had been the veil. It had looked very similar to this glowing hallway. In a flash, I remembered how I had I modulated my frequency to pass through that veil.

"Ah," I told them. "I know what to do."

I walked up to the wall and modulated my frequency, speeding it up as I had during the conference until it matched the frequency of the glowing wall. With that, I stepped through the wall to find myself standing in a cafeteria full of people in colored jumpsuits. Each one wore a single hue, but the colors in the group spanned the rainbow. The crowd gave me polite golf applause as I entered. They were effusively happy, their faces shining with congratulatory smiles. I felt so honored.

As my hosts stepped through the wall now behind me, the man placed his hand on my shoulder.

"I may be a slow learner," I told them sheepishly, "but eventually I get it."

Incredible, loving energy passed through me as I found myself awake once again and sitting up in bed.

28

Contact with Jesus

"To know the supernatural, come on over to our side for a visit. It's not scary; it's simply super! And natural."

~ Aion

The Blue Pearl, the Ashtar Command, orbs of light. My contact with Aion was challenging all my closely held beliefs. As I released them, I found myself walking through mental walls just as I had in my experience with the tall, otherworldly duo from the Ashtar Command. With this, support appeared from places I had not even considered.

Aion, sometimes I wonder, do my guides feel that I passed them over when I went to you, like I went over their heads? I don't actually know them.

No, we are all a team and are always here for you. You can certainly talk with all of your guides. They each have something unique to offer. Continue to call on the highest light and love, and that is what you will receive. After all, you called me. How did you get by my secretaries?

But seriously, you can talk with all kinds of enlightened masters beyond the veil. You can also talk directly to God and all the archangels, not to mention Jesus, called Sananda in the higher realms. But you have already spoken to him many times.

Can I receive and transmit messages and energies from these beings the way I do with you?

Yes, when you fine-tune your frequency, you can contact all of them individually. It is little different than conversing with me.

How do I do that?

Modulate your frequency by bringing the energy you want to transmit to mind. Then breathe into it and expand it, radiating out the call, the same way you call me. You already know how to do this.

Go ahead; do it now.

I am calling Jesus Sananda, the embodiment of love and transformation. Sananda, are you here?

"I am here for you, loved one. This is Jesus Sananda. Feel my energy around your heart. I am watching you closely and encouraging the shift in energy that you are experiencing. Soon, all of your talents will be put to the test.

"This is something I know about. It is humbling to serve as a conduit for Spirit's healing energy. Many will not trust you. Others will curse you and even declare you are evil. You have chosen the position of being the vessel for but not the cause of the healings. Trust in us and in your Higher Self. Regardless of the healing outcomes, remain in gratitude for the opportunity to serve humanity.

"Heal as the Holy Spirit moves you, without judging, for from the human vantage point, you cannot know another soul's agreements with Source. From my place in Spirit, these subtleties are more apparent, and yet we still practice non-interference in order to foster free will.

"Believe me, withholding judgment can be the most difficult thing you can do. But when you judge others, you end up using that same faculty to judge yourself, banishing your own consciousness from the eternal moment. You understand the pain of that separation.

"Hold compassion in your heart for those who judge you, for they know not the suffering they inflict on themselves by living outside of the sacred moment.

"All is well. Continue to open to the truth of your being. We can talk anytime, especially when you need to contact your divine heart.

"Be well."

With this, Jesus Sananda signed off. I was stunned, completely awash in this uplifting tide of love. I felt humbled to be graced with such an honor. Then I sensed Aion's familiar presence return.

That wasn't so hard, was it?

It wasn't. Sananda's energy feels so heart-centered and very compassionate.

That He is. He has a great sense of humor about it all, too. Feel free to reach out and contact other Masters and teachers. We will continue our conversation as often as you like.

How deep should my trance state be for me to clearly transmit your messages? I really want to be clear that what is coming through is truly you or others in Spirit and not my unconscious mind.

Stevie Ray, you need not be in a deep trance or any special state to receive our thought transmissions. You do, however, need to maintain a quiet mind and the intent to receive us. If your mind is running away with you, then you might consider a light trance, putting yourself a bit under in order to quiet the mind.

A placid mind bears a surface as smooth as a quiet lake in the still morning air. This state of calm stillness serves you in many ways, providing you with healing for the body, mind, and soul. A tranquil mind heals inflammation and irritation in the body, especially in the cells and the neurons of the nervous system.

Sometimes moving into a deeper state can provide additional focus and allow other beings to chime in who can contribute to your healing. They do not all have the amps, the power to get through the veil to you. We are always glad to help you and them with that when requested.

As to whether it is us or you coming through, it is safe to say it is always You. We are you and you are the One, so in effect, there is no difference. You can always think of this as transmitting messages from your Higher Self. Please do not believe that you are other than who We All Are. I know this sometimes seems like a stretch for you, but you will grow into it soon. Actually, you already are it.

Those are some pretty big shoes to fill!

No, you do not actually have to grow into our shoes. Those would be some mighty big shoes to fill. Fortunately, size doesn't matter, at least on our side.

Your so-called unconscious mind is not at all unconscious. Those in the early days of psychology who postulated this were simply unaware of this part of themselves. This part of you processes information on the soul level, translating input from the body's energetic system and from Spirit into energy and understandings you can assimilate. It is more you than the "you" whom you think you are.

In your everyday state of awareness, this would be better called heightened awareness. It includes the abilities of clairvoyance, clairaudience, clairsentience, and direct soul knowing, all aspects of your sixth sense, as well as your seventh sense of resonance and empathy. These forms of heightened sensory awareness are available to all who increase their frequency and expand their consciousness.

Don't some people want to go unconscious from time to time?

Yes, there are thoughts, feelings, and events people want to suppress, to bury away from their conscious, everyday experience.

These are better thought of as suppressed memories rather than unconsciousness.

All of this is to say that your sixth sense, your clairawareness, is more involved in translating these transmissions than your busy mind. You are also experiencing this clairawareness when dreaming or even daydreaming. You continue to think that there is something you must do in order to achieve this state of being. It is not doing but simply being that will help you arrive at your desired state. Improving your abilities requires only that you live in the natural, heightened awareness of the Now, raising your frequency each day. Vibrating at a higher rate automatically brings these abilities, which you have long denied and ignored, to the fore.

Expressing these abilities is natural, not supernatural. To know the supernatural, come on over to our side for a visit. It's not scary; it's simply super! And natural.

The question you ask speaks to some doubts that you still harbor. This is fine, not to worry. As you continue to experience our energy moving through you and healing others, you will be able to relax more and more into the knowing that we are One.

As we said before, Rome wasn't built in a day. But neither did it take millennia. This is coming to you.

You are feeling our energy now, aren't you?

Yes, I am. Thank you so much, Aion.

Simply reside in this state as often as you can. Our energy is entering you now, raising your frequency to effect a healing. Simply breathe it in, down through the top of your head, charging each chakra as you breathe into each one of them.

Do that now. Allow the energy to amplify your own energy field, then continue breathing it in, down, and through you as we increase the charge. Breathe deeply down through your core, surrendering to the vibrations and allowing them to ripple out through your body and your field. Bask in that deliciousness.

There is no need to do, only to be with it. Carry it with you. Notice any heightened awareness, any increase in your psychic senses as you go about the rest of your day. God is not only with you, God is you.

Contacting Jesus left me with an overwhelming feeling of love and compassion. The energy that had come through me was so big, so powerful that I could barely stay awake through it. I spent the next few days in a state of grace, feeling beyond honored to have the opportunity to make contact with and transmit the presence of this Master into the world.

29
A New Template

"A Creation Template is a scenario that has been deeply
discussed and lovingly developed in Spirit to serve as
a set of guiding principles for creating new
forms on Earth and elsewhere."

~ Aion

A few nights later, I took up my computer again to ask for evening guidance. From the child-like state of wonder I had been experiencing, I received from Aion a bedtime story. On the surface, it was simple as a children's book. But in the end, it would reshape my outlook on my entire life.

> Once upon a time, there was a man who lived in the woods. He led a humble life. He worked hard and cared very much for his family. To make a living, he chopped down trees with an ax. Then he used wedges to split the wood into planks for houses, tables, chairs, and everything else inside of the house. His work made him tired, so at the end of each day, he returned home to eat dinner, kiss his children goodnight, then curl up in bed beside his wife to sleep.
>
> This he did over and over again. He worked with an adz, turning rough planks smooth for wooden floors. He made shutters to protect the house against storms and shingles for a tight roof to keep out the rain. He burned branches and logs to keep his family warm. Sometimes he made beautiful furniture for his house. Many years passed this way.

In time, the woodsman had become bent over from old age and decades of hard work. He walked very slowly, hardly ever looking up at the sky. But he often looked at his house proudly. How lovely it seemed to him after all these years.

One day, he arrived home from work just as the sun was setting. When his gaze hit the chimney of his house, his eyes followed the smoke of its fireplace into the sky. He noticed how beautiful that sky was, so full of clouds and colors. The splendor of the sunset moved him so deeply that he began to cry.

Then he thought about his children who had grown up and moved away. His wife, who had also worked hard, had grown away from him, too. Even though they were still in the same house, their hearts had grown apart, and he felt alone.

"How many sunsets have I missed all these years?" he wondered. "I put all of my time, my strength, and my life's blood into this house and missed the beauty, the glory of life itself. I have a house, but I have squandered my life."

From that day on, he stopped many times a day to look at the sky, and he never missed another sunset. His heart was full, and his life was rich, through his dying day.

In the days to come, Aion's bedtime story worked its magic on me. On one hand, I sensed it was Aion's way of telling me that my life would be changing, possibly in ways that I could not yet fathom or control. Just as the couple in the story, my wife and I had grown distant. For the first time, I was admitting to myself that my relationship might come to an end.

The story also prompted me to reflect on my life as a whole. Like the woodcutter, I had been so busy making a life that I had cut myself off from my own emotions. Finally I was ready to abandon my plans and enjoy the beauty around me.

From this place of openness and surrender, I experienced a lucid dream unlike any other. Even visitations from Aion had not been as vivid or detailed as the Creation Template dream.

Last night I dreamed continually of creating a spiritual community, including a college with a campus, a strong set of supporting business cooperatives, and a broadcasting studio as an active outreach for like-minded souls. What was that about?

God blesses you, Stevie Ray. You received a Creation Template, a series of ideas that serve as instructions for creating. A Creation Template is a scenario that has been deeply discussed and lovingly developed in Spirit to serve as a set of guiding principles for creating new forms on Earth and elsewhere.

The template you received could serve as a new type of social structure, reflecting energy shifts already underway in the planet's transformation. New ways of organizing people around healing, joy, inspiration, and compassion as well as new ideas for handling money exchange, food, and energy sustainability are all built into that template. Do you remember it?

It made such a strong impression in me that it would be hard to forget.

The template seemed to come in a series of waves, each one with an additional layer of information. Each new wave overlaid the previous one with more auditory instructions, visual images, and emotional experiences. I felt a sense of momentum as the template built. It seemed like hours passed, though I couldn't keep track of time.

Strangely, I feel like I have always known this new idea.

Actually, you have—or rather, this new and improved version of you has. This you has chosen a new strand of possibility to follow.

What does this mean for me?

You mean WIIFM, "What's in it for me?" Or, "What is my responsibility regarding this new revelation?"

I mean, what does this imply I have to do?

Relax. There is no doing required, no need to feel over-responsible about this. It simply means your life is unfolding as it will. This template lies along one string of the future you that you currently are creating.

Remember, there are no "shoulds" here. But we in Spirit always like to plant new seeds as resources for humans to use in their development. If the template inspires you, great! If not, that's fine. Release it. Just knowing and experiencing it will give you a deeper understanding of how to proceed in community building.

My heart longs for the kind of conscious, caring, creative community life the template laid out. It would be Heaven on Earth.

Indeed. And now you have this inspiration in your heart. Continue on your current path, and this feeling will grow, illuminating your days and nights.

Templates serve as beacons of light ahead on a soul's path of creation. It is always up to the soul to take the next step toward that light. You can choose another string to follow at any time or not.

How do I bring all this to life?

Write the business plan and create it in reality. There is no need to involve lots of people since you are the one who received the template. Simply allow the seed idea to sprout and grow.

You will recognize what you must do as the need arises. Input from others will be useful, but do not let it distract you from what you know from the template. Trust that knowing, and hold the vision. Take one step at a time, manifesting the vision in your plane of reality.

We will support you every step of the way with grace. Grace is a divine flow of energy that lubricates reality, reducing and even eliminating the friction that can accompany creation on your planet. Grace helps by aligning energies from all corners of the multiverse, clearing the way for creation. It induces serendipity and happenstance, influencing so-called chance and increasing the odds of successful manifestation. Grace always operates in accordance with free will while honoring the multi-dimensional strings of possibility that extend to every soul. In this way, seemingly random happenings can coalesce into a magnificent, powerful creation.

By holding the vision of the template, you act as a conduit for grace to flow into reality. As you step into the template, grace will assist its emergence into your world. Of course, you must request it, but once invited, grace will pull a few strings, and your dream becomes a reality, gracefully!

What happens if I choose to follow this string, creating the template?

What do you feel would happen?

I feel my life would blossom. I can't imagine a more beautiful, fulfilling way to live. It's all the best aspects of a university, a startup company, a vibrant eco-village, and a contemplative community.

There you go. We encourage you to keep asking questions and finding the answers within. We love playing the role of psycho-therapist. The Soul Guardians guard more than inter-dimensional, space-time creation. They also help you with your mental health. Nurturing consciousness is the number one responsibility.

As you form the next question in your mind, notice the answer appearing simultaneously.

You're right! The answer is immediately there. Why didn't I notice this before?

As the "you before," you were vibrating at a different frequency and had not established such a secure link to ours. The same opportunity was there, of course, but you had not stepped into it.

Each breath, each thought or feeling can propel you into the "next you" along the string of probability you have chosen. This does not have to be a sequence of steps. You can take leaps and bounds by opening to conscious reception of templates for your path.

Will the templates change as the string I choose changes?

Yes, of course the templates will change as you choose new tangents to follow. Did you check within for the answer as you formulated the question?

Oh, no, I did not. Thanks for reminding me.

You're welcome. We will always encourage you to remember what you already know. And it is always OK to ask.

Aion, what else do I already know? How can I remember it?

Those are important questions. Let's take the second question first, because if you can remember how to remember, the first question is unnecessary.

Just understand, once you remember, it is difficult to forget again. The knowledge is yours to integrate into your life choices.

I understand. You're saying remembering what I know will change me forever.

It will change you in this string of a lifetime, and those changes will ripple out to the "you" in every dimension. I sense your acceptance of this, along with a request for more support from us.

Take a few deep breaths and clear your energetic flow. Loosen up and consciously relax.

Let's go on a little trip together. I will be at your side the entire way. If you want to return at any time to your present state of being, just ask, and you will be back to it instantly and comfortably. We ask for the highest protection for your soul. Only that which is of love and light, for your highest good, can touch your consciousness.

Breathe down through the top of your head. Fill your field with golden shower of energy. Hold the request, "Please help me remember how to remember that which I already know." Repeat it as you continue to wait for your memories to surface.

I am remembering experiences with Spirit, fragments of past lives, my own birth, merging with the white light. Here is what I remember.

* I can die, merge with the light, return, and do it again.
* I can heal by channeling the golden hands of Spirit.
* I have visited the Ashtar Command and passed through the ship's walls.
* I can and do travel consciously out of my body.
* I can merge with God and another through tantric sexual union.
* I am a soul pilot, transporting the newly dead to their rest and recovery places in the universe.
* I know how to pass through time and space by using my imagination.
* I remember how to build, care for, and protect a tribe.
* I know how to create and re-create my life at a higher frequency.
* I know how to transmit the healing energy of Spirit.
* I know how to talk with God, Jesus, and Spirit.
* I know how to wake up in other dimensions.
* I know I have seen and experienced the Rupa, the Blue Pearl.

I accept all these remembrances as my knowing, a part of me, the Here-and-Now Stevie Ray. I will no longer write them off as just interesting stories, but own them as who I am and what I know. I accept my soul knowing.

I now remember how to remember what I already know. And there is so much more that I know.

There, you see, you are new again, re-newed. How do you feel?

I feel expanded and humbled. I also understand that this knowing is just the slightest touch of your reality. And I know your reality is Real and is now my reality, too. I feel I can bring much more of me into the game, into my present.

You can if you so choose. So now, knowing all this, what does that make you?

I am undeniably a divine being.

30

So Create!

*"Creating is God's work and play, and every consciousness
contributes to the generation of our multiple realities."*

~ Aion

After the Creation Template download for community, my energy healing work with clients took on a new urgency for me. With Aion's guidance, I would prepare for clients before they arrived with the mindset that each person coming to me was a part of the community for which my soul had been longing.

Aion, I have been preparing for a healing session on creativity, self-expression, and clearing the throat chakra. I would love to have your instruction in these topics.

Creation is one of my favorite topics. This is something all souls participate in equally, though most don't recognize it. Creating is God's work and play, and every consciousness contributes to the generation of our multiple realities.

You are familiar with all kinds of energy, and scientists are making noble efforts to understand the various frequencies, charges, and behaviors of currently detectable energy. Waves, particles, and even the spin of massless energies don't begin to cover the inventive variations of God's creation.

What is more important, though, is to understand that it all begins as a thought. Thoughts have energy, and thus, frequency, amplitude, and persistence. On our side, we can see thoughts radiating out in all directions from their point of origin. Some thoughts can cross limitless space and multiple dimensions.

Thoughts, as energy, interact with each other, sometimes amplifying and sometimes cancelling each other out, like ripples from two stones thrown into a pond. Thoughts change the medium through which they pass. That medium can be you, the air and space around you, other people, and even the very ethers of the universe.

All thoughts create. From art and architecture, to healing body and soul, to wrangling subatomic particles—all are creative acts of thought. Yes, thoughts can impact the stars, bend space, and void time. Time itself is just a thought, after all, and an afterthought at that! Thought is faster than light and more powerful than gravity. Such is the magnificence of creative thought from Source.

Creativity begins as thought. Thoughts are formed by a consciousness. The impact and creative effectiveness of the thought are determined by the frequency and amplitude of the consciousness generating the thought. When we are healing, sealing, and integrating a person's energy field, we are, of course, also expanding their consciousness. Energy and consciousness are inextricably linked. The more you expand your consciousness, the stronger your receptivity to the Source of All Ideas becomes. This increases your creative potential, to say the least.

Creativity comes alive with the connection to Spirit. In fact, co-creation, tapping into inspiration from Spirit and adding your own ideas to create a new expression of consciousness, is the highest form of creativity. You might invent a unique expression or just one that is new to you, but you are creating nonetheless.

At the same time, ideas from almost any level of consciousness can move from formless thought into form. This can work for the good or ill of an individual or for all beings on the planet. Ideas like family, community, money, government, or war all manifest through the collective consciousness and free will of all. As the consciousness on Earth shifts, so does the nature of these institutions.

All souls are expressed from Source. All that love, all that divine intelligence and power are you. Just as Source expressed you, you can express yourself in creativity. That expression helps you know consciousness, which is the whole point of creation. You are here to conceive, and I don't just mean populating the planet.

Ideas manifest through the will, the intent of the soul. The more you are aligned to Source at the soul level, the easier it is to create or express. If you want to help people create or to better express ideas, help them experience their direct connection to Spirit. By integrating their souls, their consciousness expands and can reach across the veil to the Divine Idea. There is no greater inspiration, no greater motivation to create than that.

How does creating with thought square with being without thought, present in the Now?

Ah, another paradox. Now we are getting somewhere!

We are speaking of thought forms here, of pure ideation and divine conception. These originate in whispers from Spirit, not the shouting of ego mind. The muse is not amused by the ego mind. Only by quieting that chatter and creating space between thoughts does reception become possible.

Being in the moment opens the soul to inspiration from Spirit. It awakens creativity, the birthright of all beings. When thoughts of yourself cease, thoughts from your Higher Self begin.

So create!

Sometimes I felt an idea arose from divine inspiration, directing me to a job or along a particular career, only to find out it was not a good fit for me. Was I missing something in the guidance? Was I just in my mind? What happened?

Center yourself and think back through all the jobs and career changes you have been through since you started working. In each case, remember why you made a change. What pattern do you notice?

In each case, I wanted and asked for a change, and I received it. Then I pursued the new line of work until I stopped enjoying it. Either I was successful but bored with it, found I was not really good at it, or just stopped marketing until my business faded away because I couldn't bring myself to continue in that line of work.

Twice I consciously set out on a new course altogether. Each time, I moved into a healing-oriented role for a few years, then I left it. Now, so many years later, I am returning to that role once again. It feels like such a relief.

Each time you returned to a healing modality, you felt relieved. This satisfied something in your soul that was calling to you. It is your calling that you ignored each time you left that field, so you felt dissatisfied on a deep level, even when you were financially successful doing something else.

How long have you known you were a healer?

Forever, simply forever. Aion, what else should I offer?

What the earth plane needs now is a new way for people to interact that will generate healing, education, and inspiration. Imagine you are a radio tower beaming the thoughts, insights, and feelings from the spiritual experiences you have, awake or asleep. Imagine if all light workers, acting as light bridges between the worlds, could do the same. How powerful a force for change would that be? The sheer magnitude of the wave of love would be like a tsunami of healing washing over the earth.

So offer what you know. Set up an interactive broadcasting capability and invite all kinds of people to participate. Generate excitement for living in bliss, in the Here and Now, creating Heaven on Earth. Teach that it is not as important to get what you want as to be Who You Are.

People are afraid to follow their guidance. The straight and narrow way has them. It will take a strong, loving influence and much grace to help them let go and move into what they already know. Once grace tips the scale, the momentum of soul healing and integration will carry them into a new and present reality. Then they, too, can join forces with the light workers and spirit beings bringing this glorious transformation to Earth.

My main message is that now all souls can come of age, fully entering into their birthright as expressions of Source. The veil is thinning, making this is an opportunity not to miss. But, of course, all souls have free will.

Truly accepting your God-ness and vibrating in that frequency will transform life and contribute to the God Fund, that ever-growing radiance of divine light. Acceptance of your Higher Self means vibrating with the love and healing energy of the angels and archangels, becoming the One. It requires letting go of fear, releasing self-identification, and embracing the expansive, loving energy of Source, for humankind is no less than All That.

But to accept the Higher Self, the limited self must transform, and that feels a lot like dying. For most people, ego death is death, the same thing as passing over, which scares them. We are here to say that by elevating frequency, you can have it all—living in the body while enjoying all the benefits and bliss available on the other side.

For that to happen, all the fear and limiting beliefs must fall away. This feels like a big risk to the ego. "Why should I believe the wild ravings of an ancient, disembodied entity who never incarnated in the first place?" your ego asks.

But I am not asking anyone to believe. I am asking all those for whom the separation has become unbearable to directly experience the healing energy of Spirit and to know the truth of the Higher Self. From that state, there is no doubt or fear because the Higher Self knows no separation, only joy, love, and the celebration of consciousness experiencing Itself.

This is why we are making this special offer to those who can see, hear, and feel the whispering of the soul, the touch of Spirit upon them. Theirs can be the bliss of union with Source if only they can accept who they Are.

The community of light we are asking you to grow will be big enough to contain many teachers and masters. All will have their own way of pursuing and disseminating the truth. There are as many paths as there are souls, and having many teachers makes finding a fit for each student an easier task. Your role is to act as the center of the circle, maintaining the Spirit connection that is the energetic core of the group. Maintaining integrity, clarity, collaboration, community, and joy will keep the group expanding and deepening. It will take egoless leadership and a strong connection to Spirit. Yes, you can!

Please take our offer of help for establishing conscious, caring, creative community seriously. By this we mean, take our love, appreciation, and guidance to heart. Allow us to light up your heart and illuminate the path, which is an endless circle of expanding consciousness. Each turn about this circle raises the frequency of all beings. Seen from far above, you could say that the ever-rising, ever-widening circle is actually a spiral, a 3-D metaphor that arises naturally from our celestial viewpoint.

Somehow, I feel I already know how to do this.

Yes, you already know how, though you have never done it before. This is part of your inner knowing emerging at your call.

Is this a knowing from a past life?

There is no past, only the present in multiple dimensions. You are still you in all of them, and the knowledge from them is available to you when you are vibrating at a matching frequency. Modulating your frequency is the key to what might be called time travel, if time actually existed. You can go forward and backward, following strings of possibility that radiate outward from the Now. Each dimension carries the very same unique spark of you expressed from Source.

One spark, multiple yous. Wrap your understanding around that!

31

The Holy Spirit

"The Holy Spirit is the wind that stirs souls, gathering
them in inspiration and then dispersing them
on their paths back to Source."

~ Aion

Aion, what is next for me?

Be prepared, Boy Scout. Stay centered and stay tuned. So much will be coming at once that your life will be full to over-brimming. To be ready, sharpen your seven senses, and hone your energy practice to a fine edge. Learn to wield the blade of awareness, cutting through attachment and self-identification. We are annealing your steel for strength and flexibility.

Or to use a feminine metaphor, be the vessel of our divine love. Allow our grace to move you in the dance of creativity. Attune your senses to the angelic communication around you, and nurture the Spirit within you. Open your consciousness to that which flows through you, and release all that is not the Highest You.

Both your male and female aspects will serve you in the period to come.

What is coming?

Again and again, you will be asked to speak of your personal experience, our conversations, and the soul healings. Many asking will have had little personal contact with Spirit and will lack under-standing. Be patient and gentle with them in spite of their manner in asking. Remember, this is not about you, so don't take it per-sonally. We, the Beings of Light and the Soul Guardians, are always with you and will help you through the process.

This role is one I have yearned for, prayed for, and long awaited. I'm happy to be your front man. Your support for me is unwavering.

Yes, it is, and we rejoice in your willingness to speak to those who will listen. For those who will not, let them be. You have more than enough to do in reaching out to all those who are ready to hear. The circle will grow exponentially. There will be circles within circles within circles, and at the center will be the experience of Spirit energy flowing through all those who serve as bridges be-tween worlds.

Not to worry. Many will share this opportunity to bring trans-formation to light.

I believe you, and this is hard to imagine as I sit here quietly in my living room, listening to the wind stir the leaves in the yard.

No need to imagine. The Holy Spirit is the wind that stirs souls, gathering them in inspiration and then dispersing them on their paths back to Source.

I was nervous to even consider the next question that rose in my mind. But I had to ask.

Aion, are you the Holy Spirit?

I am. I am the Breath of God.

I was astounded. Speechless.

Throughout my childhood, I had learned about the Holy Spirit as a part of the Christian Holy Trinity: the Father, the Son, and the Holy Ghost. Yes, Aion had revealed to me that he was Ra, Brahma, and others. But none of these had landed in the same way for me. The Holy Spirit was not just an angel speaking on God's behalf, a being dreamed up by humans to represent God, or even a force radiating from God. The teaching from the catechism went, "No one comprehends the thoughts of God except the Spirit of God." The Holy Spirit was God Himself. THE God. And when God as the Holy Spirit spoke, it was with tongues of fire, to prophets and apostles—people who changed the course of history. Not to someone like me.

I reached for words like fumbling for my glasses in the dark without finding them.

Hello, Stevie Ray, are you still there? Can you hear me now?

I could hear Aion, but I was completely blown away. Was THE Holy Spirit actually communicating directly with me, or had I simply become delusional?

Breathe a bit. Spiritus means breath. Breath brings inspiration. You become in spiritus, inspired by Spirit.

I did my best to breathe in what Aion had just revealed. But I was having a hard time. I ended the session abruptly, unable to continue. Three days passed before I worked up the nerve to sit down again with my computer to receive insight from... THE Holy Spirit.

I'm still trying to accept the idea that you are the Holy Spirit. Does this mean the Holy Spirit has descended upon me as it was visited upon the apostles?

You have been enjoying our little visits, have you not? Do you feel descended upon?

I am deeply moved and completely transformed by our visits. I wouldn't say, "descended upon." That's just the language of the Bible that I recall. It is more like feeling filled by the energy of Spirit, uplifted by bliss, encouraged to merge and enter into the highest vibration of love and wisdom. My experience of our connection and conversation is divine.

So what's the problem? Why the shock and awe?

I have always assumed this kind of visitation could only happen to apostles, disciples, saints, bodhisattvas, and spiritual adepts. I'm just a guy. I am in no way holy, divine, or even disciplined for that matter.

Take a deep breath and listen to yourself. What do you hear?

I hear a guy denying his spiritual wisdom, demeaning his direct experience of God, and judging himself just like his authoritarian father judged him. Ouch.

Judgments also hurt those who judge. You can let yourself off the not-good-enough hook now simply by breathing in and reaching out for our inspiration.

Loving yourself is actually loving your Divine Self. You cannot love others without first loving yourself. By experiencing your true spiritual nature and accepting the broad sweep of your developing consciousness, you will realize you have been using a very limited scope of concepts to judge yourself.

Compassion begins with you. As you accept yourself, you begin to see Self in all beings. Knowing and respecting your Self in all its aspects, what you label both positive and negative, lays the foundation for activating the seventh sense of resonance and empathy.

Empathy creates synergy. It is a union of two or more souls, yet each soul retains its unique spark. Empathetic beings are able to share their wisdom, insights and experiences to benefit all of a similar frequency. Your empathy yields compassion, forgiveness, and healing for all. You can see how judging yourself or others impairs this experience.

Recognize the judgment in the moment, dissolve it with loving energy, and let it go. It takes no time at all, and then you are back in the flow. Eventually, with practice of calling upon the Breath of God, you will heal the judgments and seal the leaks they cause in your field.

I guess this means it is time for me to live up to my own spiritual expectations.

Ah, where to start? Let's start with: No.

No, you are not here to live up to expectations, because there are none, except those you either created for yourself or assumed from your upbringing. When I say you are off the hook, it is because there is no hook. You can relax, Charlie. No one is trying to land and filet you. You are free to swim about in the sea of consciousness.

Didn't I make a contract with God before I incarnated about achieving certain realizations, some milestones for spiritual growth?

You received suggestions and reflections from your soul panel, of which I am a part.

In every moment, you are guided, nudged toward the realizations you chose to pursue in this lifetime, because you asked for it. Life is a creative exploration of consciousness. You can exercise free will at any point to express your unique awareness.

There is no contract. There is only becoming in the moment. This notion of expectations and a covenant with each soul regarding how to be during a lifetime is false. The covenant is one of our total support for you in whatever path you choose on your journey back to Source. And we say it starts with "no" because this is the energy of separation needed to cut the cords of attachment to the not-good-enough aspect of your soul.

You're thinking Spirit is only about saying yes, acceptance, and dissolving the ego-mind. But that's not the half of it. To speak with One Voice, a soul needs both a strong "yes" and a strong "no." This is the ability to discern.

Discernment demands discrimination between what resonates with your highest frequency and what does not. This doesn't mean judging that which you are not, because You Are Everything. And we already know that judging yourself is painful, so we would not want you to do that to yourself.

The paradox is to love everything but be only that which you truly are, that which resonates with your frequency. There can be many notes in a chord but not all notes will resonate in it. Still, every note can find a chord in which to resonate. Just as certain chords fit in a specific musical key, beings experiencing resonant frequencies will feel they fit together. They are One in the Spirit. Again, it is a matter of fit, not fault.

So we say, put away your whip. Stop flagellating yourself and start congratulating yourself instead. With every conscious breath, flow into the moment and experience your divine Self. You are plenty God enough!

Yes, yes, yes! Yes, I can. Yes, I will. Yes, I AM!

And so be it. So, be it!

Afterward

This book chronicles my first six months of conversations with Aion, also known as the Holy Spirit. But the journey I began then continues to surprise, delight, and inspire me. Every day I am learning more about what it means to be God enough.

As a result, my continuing saga is more than I could ever fit into the pages of a single book. I have received enough guidance from Aion since that first day of our conversations on April 19, 2009, to make this one volume seem like a single star in the night sky. Additional books will follow, along with a variety of other offerings to illuminate the path for those who aspire to serve as a bridge between worlds.

And the rest of the story? As Aion taught me, each of us is a living book, created and shaped by thousands of encounters over many lifetimes. If you feel moved, touched, or called by this work in any way, then the story of Aion continues in you. Where will you be guided? What insights await you from Source? What tales will you have to tell as you continue your voyage Home?

The Unified Field Meditation is the core practice of the teachings of Aion. For a free audio version of this practice, along with more detailed instructions, visit:
www.StevieRayMcHugh.com

I like the book?
Your voice counts! Please review the book on Amazon so that even more people can explore life as God Enough.

Index of Practices

At its heart, this book is a collection of practical wisdom. In my conversations with Aion, I also received a number of repeatable practices, both long and short, that anyone could use to expand in consciousness. The list below is by no means exhaustive, but rather, an attempt to highlight some of the more ready-to-use practices from Aion.

How would your life change if you lived like You Are God Enough?

- Facing a tough transition?
- Unsure about your next step?
- Feeling stuck or alone on your path?

Get clear, get energized, get free!

Schedule a complimentary session with me today to explore the joy of living your purpose.

 Rise above struggle and self-doubt by contacting your own guidance. Manifest your dreams with the support of a spiritual mentor, psychic, psychotherapist, and inspired business coach with more than 30 years of experience.

I have coached hundreds in transition, and I walk this road myself every day.

In my work, I focus on spiritual guidance AND practical, boots-on-the-ground wisdom.

Visit StevieRayMcHugh.com and take a leap toward your Future's Future Self.